Interpreting
Hebrew
Poetry

Interpreting Hebrew Poetry

by
DAVID L. PETERSEN and
KENT HAROLD RICHARDS

FORTRESS PRESS
Minneapolis

INTERPRETING HEBREW POETRY

Library of Congress Cataloging-in-Publication Data

Petersen, David L.
    Interpreting Hebrew poetry / by David L. Petersen and Kent Harold
Richards.
      p.   cm.—(Guides to biblical scholarship)
    Includes bibliographical references and indexes.
    ISBN 0-8006-2625-7 (alk. paper) :
    1. Hebrew poetry, Biblical—History and criticism.   2. Bible.
O.T.—Language, style. 3. Hebrew language—Parallelism.
I. Richards, Kent Harold, 1939– . II. Title. III. Series.
BS1405.2.P48   1992
892.4′1109—dc20   92-7934
                                                                CIP

Manufactured in the U.S.A.   AF 1-2625

6   7   8   9   10   11

Contents

Editor's Foreword

It is hardly possible to understand the Hebrew Bible without coming to terms with Hebrew poetry. Although unlike the poetry of modern Western languages in many important respects, Hebrew poetry is dense, rich, and often enigmatic language that calls for and evokes careful reading.

Until quite recently, however, biblical scholars felt confident about their understanding of most of the basic features of Hebrew poetry. But a number of important proposals have appeared that call older theories into question, making it clear that this language is not as simple as it appeared to be only a decade ago. The goal of this volume is to provide a guide both to the recent scholarly discussion and to understanding Hebrew poetry itself.

Petersen and Richards begin with the problems of definition, pointing out that it is not always easy to distinguish poetry from prose in the Hebrew Bible. Although virtually all modern translations of the Bible—unlike the earliest translations such as the Authorized Version—indicate the presence of poetry by the way the lines are set on the page, decisions about what is and is not poetry are subject to debate and disagreement. Petersen and Richards consider parallelism and meter, long taken to be the main characteristics of Hebrew poetry. They summarize and evaluate the major insights into these issues from the time of Bishop Robert Lowth and other early scholars to recent discussions, some of which call into question parallelism of lines as the distinctive mark of poetry. They point out both the usefulness and the limitations of theories of meter, preferring to speak in terms of rhythm.

In addition to these traditional topics in the analysis of Hebrew poetry, Petersen and Richards take up some of the recent literary critical discussions of Hebrew poetics, the theory and practice of understanding poetic literature. They introduce some of the features of Hebrew poetic style, including stylistic devices, such as inclusios, chiastic structures, plays on words, and assonance.

The authors illustrate some of the problems and possible solutions with examples taken from different types of biblical poetry. The reader of the Hebrew Bible, including in its English translations, is thus enabled to recognize and understand more of the depth and richness of its poetic expression.

Gene M. Tucker
Emory University

Abbreviations

AB	Anchor Bible
BASOR	*Bulletin of the American Schools of Oriental Research*
BHK	*Biblia Hebraica Württembergensia*
BHS	*Biblia Hebraica Stuttgartensia*
Bib	*Biblica*
BKAT	Biblischer Kommentar, Altes Testament
BibOr	Biblica et orientalia
BZ	*Biblische Zeitschrift*
CBCNEB	Cambridge Bible Commentary on the New English Bible
CBQ	*Catholic Biblical Quarterly*
CTM	*Calwer Theologische Monographien*
FOTL	Forms of the Old Testament Literature
GBS.OTS	Guides to Biblical Scholarship. Old Testament Series
GNB	Good News Bible
HBC	*Harper's Bible Commentary*
HBD	*Harper's Bible Dictionary*
HKAT	Handkommentar zum Alten Testament
HSM	Harvard Semitic Monographs
HTR	*Harvard Theological Review*
ICC	International Critical Commentary
IDB	*Interpreter's Dictionary of the Bible*
ISBL	Indiana Studies in Biblical Literature
JAOS	*Journal of the American Oriental Society*
JBL	*Journal of Biblical Literature*
JETS	*Journal of the Evangelical Theological Society*
JQR	*Jewish Quarterly Review*
JSOT	*Journal for the Study of the Old Testament*
JSOTSS	JSOT Supplement Series

MT	Masoretic text
NAB	New American Bible
NCBC	New Century Bible Commentary
NIV	New International Version
NJB	New Jerusalem Bible
NRSV	New Revised Standard Version
OTL	Old Testament Library
PHPT	*The Princeton Handbook of Poetic Terms*
RB	*Revue Biblique*
RSV	Revised Standard Version
SBLDS	Society of Biblical Literature, Dissertation Series
SBT	Studies in Biblical Theology
TANAKH	A New Translation of the Holy Scripture According to the Traditional Hebrew Text
TZ	*Theologische Zeitschrift*
UF	*Ugarit Forschungen*
VT	*Vetus Testamentum*
VTSup	Vetus Testamentum, Supplements
WBC	Word Biblical Commentary
WMANT	Wissenschaftliche Monographien zum Alten und Neuen Testament
ZAW	*Zeitschrift für die alttestamentliche Wissenschaft*
*	Author's translation

1
Understanding Hebrew Poetry

Virtually all texts from the ancient Near Eastern Bronze, Iron, and Persian ages present the reader with difficulties. Even when translated, literature from these periods is so different from the literature to which the contemporary reader is accustomed that various introductory matters must be addressed in order to make that literature understandable. This judgment applies to ancient prose as well as to ancient poetry. Just as with contemporary literature, however, poetry presents the reader with special difficulties. Poetry typically contains denser and richer language than does prose, even well-wrought prose, of the same period and sensibility.

Evidence of such difficulty in biblical poetry is easily presented. One of the brief essays provided by the editors of *The New Oxford Annotated Bible* is entitled "Characteristics of Hebrew Poetry." There is no analogous piece entitled "Characteristics of Hebrew Prose," although such an essay could be written. In a related vein, among the general essays in *The Literary Guide to the Bible* is a section entitled "The Characteristics of Ancient Hebrew Poetry."[1] Again, there is no corresponding section on Hebrew prose. In these two volumes and the essays they devote to Hebrew poetry, the editors provide evidence of their judgment that the reader of the Bible encounters special difficulties when reading ancient Hebrew poetry. It is a judgment with which we agree.[2]

Most general treatments of ancient Hebrew poetry emphasize two essential characteristics: parallelism and meter.[3] As a result of recent scholarly developments, such treatments that use the categories of meter and parallelism as traditionally understood no longer suffice. To speak of parallelism and meter, assuming that there is a scholarly consensus about the definitions or even the existence of these phenomena

1

in Hebrew, would mislead the reader. Such a consensus no longer exists. Consequently, we provide this volume in order to explain why the old consensus has been laid aside and to suggest the groundwork for a new consensus, one based on recent linguistic and literary study of Hebrew poetry and on theories about poetry in all languages.

DEFINITION

Attempts to define Hebrew poetry are, in principle, no more difficult or simple than defining the poetry of any other language. However, since parallelism has usually been viewed as the single distinguishing characteristic of Hebrew poetry, scholars have focused on it. They have not regularly examined other features of that literary corpus in the same way that those who study English poetry treat the diverse features of that language's poetry. It is commonplace for readers of English poetry to study rhythm or meter, rhyme, stanzaic structure, and symbolism as important elements in English-language poetry. Few, however, have devoted attention to these or similar aspects of Hebrew poetry. As a result, important features that constitute Hebrew poetry have not been discussed.

Even discussions of English poetry reveal numerous critical and theoretical debates about what it is that makes English poetry poetic. This situation obtains even more so for Hebrew poetry. The lack of a consensus need not, however, prevent the reader from reading and understanding Hebrew poetry; it simply means that one could hold only a tentative notion about its essential nature while reading it.

In our judgment, it is useful to hold such tentative notions even about the fundamental features of Hebrew poetry. Here we need to make a distinction between what is necessary and what is helpful. We may do so by using an analogy drawn from the world of music. Any number of people have heard a sonata. Those who have studied neither music theory nor the history of music may well enjoy the performance or the recording of the sonata. They can perceive whether the artist plays well, whether the piece is interpreted in a suitable way. However, the person who has studied music theory is in a better position to understand the music fully, namely, to know something about the sonata structure and about the way in which that music might best be interpreted.

The situation with reading Hebrew poetry is analogous but more complex. One can read Hebrew poems in translation—for example, those in the Song of Songs—and enjoy them. If the reader is experienced in reading literature, especially poetry, then that individual will be able to understand something about the poems, such as their rich pastoral imagery. However, the person who has some basic knowledge of the essential features of Hebrew poetry has a decided advantage because that reader will be attuned to the fundamental features of rhythm, parallelism, and the other stylistic features that are hallmarks of Hebrew poetry. Such an understanding is essential for a fuller comprehension of that literature.

At this point, however, the analogy with music breaks down, since our understanding of the theory of Hebrew poetry is much less precise than is our understanding of the sonata form. As a result, although some understanding of Hebrew poetry is apposite, one must hold those theories lightly when reading Hebrew verse.

PROBLEMS

The antiquity of Hebrew poetry presents a series of problems that one does not confront when studying or reading modern poetry. First, there are no extant discussions from antiquity about poetic theory within Hebrew or, for that matter, any other ancient Semitic language. Second, and in a related vein, our understandings of some poetic forms and poetic subdivisions, for example, stanzas, are sometimes imprecise. Our handicap here is most evident when we read the psalms. In the titles that introduce many of the psalms, there are Hebrew words that seem to indicate something about the kind of poetry in the psalm or, alternately, something about the type of musical accompaniment appropriate for that poem. For example, Psalm 32 is labeled a *maśkîl*, Psalm 16 a *miktām*. Knowledge of the meaning of these rubrics would tell us something significant about religious poetry in the Old Testament. So also the mysterious *selāh*, which recurs throughout the Psalter, defies convincing explanation. If one understood the significance of this term in its seventy-one occurrences in the Book of Psalms and three occurrences in Habakkuk, then one would know considerably more about the structure and performance of these texts than is currently known. Psalm 3, for example, uses the term three times in fewer than ten verses.[4] At the moment, the significance of such terms, and thus their contribution to an understanding of Hebrew poetry, are lost in the mists of antiquity.

Second, and more important, since we have no original texts, it is not obvious how the poems were structured. Our lack of knowledge here involves both the length and the configuration of the individual

3

poetic lines and the putative existence of stanzas. The earliest biblical manuscripts for a poetic text—for example, the Isaiah scrolls from Qumran—do not present texts in the poetic forms that we are accustomed to seeing in current editions of the Bible. In these texts—the NRSV and the NIV among them—poetry is printed in a special fashion. To put it simplistically, modern translations print poetry with extra white space and with many parallel lines. One may note this by comparing Exodus 14 with Exodus 15 in any modern translation. Ancient biblical manuscripts themselves do not inform us about how these poetic texts should be printed. This formatting decision involves significant judgments about the structure of Hebrew poetry. For example, in one of the Dead Sea Scroll manuscripts of Isaiah (1QIsaᵃ), the first clause in Isa. 5:7 is written in no way different from prose sections in that scroll. In the NRSV, the text is formatted in the following way:

> For the vineyard of the LORD of hosts
> is the house of Israel,

By contrast, GNB prints it the following way:

> Israel is the vineyard of the
> LORD Almighty;

NAB does the following:

> The vineyard of the LORD of
> hosts is the house of Israel,

These three respected translations construe the line division of the poetry in three different ways. This is for good reason, since the Hebrew text itself does not provide information about how the lines should be divided.

This issue of lineation, or the stichometric division of the text, is not even satisfactorily addressed by the critical editions of the Hebrew Bible. Biblical scholars have had available either the *Biblia Hebraica Württembergensia* (BHK), published in 1937, or *Biblia Hebraica Stuttgartensia* (BHS), published in 1983. Stichometric divisions of Hebrew poetry vary considerably between these two editions. For example, in the case of Isa. 5:7, the first line in Hebrew reads (our translation) according to BHS, "Indeed, the vineyard of Yahweh of Hosts (is) the house of Israel." *BHS* construes these words to comprise one long line, an understanding different from all the modern translations cited above. *BHK*, by contrast, prints these words as if they comprised "parallel" lines:

> Indeed the vineyard of Yahweh of Hosts
> the house of Israel.

The verb "is" is understood and not written in the Hebrew text. To make matters more complicated, *BHK* and *BHS* even differ in their understandings about whether a particular text is prose or poetry. So, for example, Isa. 4:2 is printed as poetry in *BHK* and as prose in *BHS*. This debate is preserved as well in modern translations. NIV views Isa. 4:2, along with *BHS*, as prose; TANAKH and NAB, along with *BHK*, view it as poetry. To be sure, these matters involving the stichometric division of the text do not prevent readers from understanding the poem at a basic level. However, this disagreement about the division of the poetic lines, and even about whether or not a text is poetic, provides graphic evidence about the state of our knowledge (cf. pp. 13–14; 23–24 below).

This lack of knowledge about the theory and structure of Hebrew poetry is made even more problematic by the state of the texts that preserve classical Hebrew poems. They are obviously not the original autographs, that is, the actual copies that the ancient poets wrote. Nor do we have any reason to think that any Hebrew manuscripts reproduce accurately the autographs. Rather, they are copies of copies, most made several centuries after the original poems were composed. In the long process of transmission, either in oral or in written form, numerous changes occur in poetic texts. Even in English poetry changes occur, such as the shift in Thomas Gray's "Elegy Written in a Country Churchyard," where the phrase "sacred bower" sometimes appears in the third quatrain for the far more provocative "secret bower."[5]

Third, the form of the language in Hebrew poems is not always certain. The orthography, or spelling, present in the standard, critical editions of the Hebrew Bible represents the final stage in a long series of developments. So, when one attempts to determine the rhythm of a Hebrew poem, one must remember that the Masoretic text's vocalization includes a phonology, a system of sounds, that may not reflect the poem's original form. Adding to, subtracting from, or revising the sound and spelling of a word or line affects fundamentally the way it works rhythmically. To be sure, all languages, including English, undergo change over time. However, the reader of English poetry perceives readily the differences between Beowulf, Shakespeare, and Pound. Such is not the case with readers of the Old Testament, even with those who read the text in Hebrew. These changes, which reflect shifts in the Hebrew language, create special problems for the student of Hebrew poetry.

A fourth problem confronting the study of Hebrew poetry is the isolation of the study of this ancient poetry from the study of non Semitic poetry. As a result, the work of those who theorize critically about poetry in English and other languages has not regularly informed the analysis of Hebrew poetry. There are a number of reasons for this situation. Primary among them is Robert Lowth's notion of parallelism, which has shaped the analysis of Hebrew poetry.[6] He took parallelism to be the dominant feature of Hebrew verse, a view that has often led to the conviction that Hebrew poetry was distinct from most other kinds of poetry. No modern English poetry, for example, is understood to have parallelism as "the only determinant of form."[7] In fact, the definition of parallelism in *The Princeton Handbook of Poetic Terms* focuses the discussion upon the notion of biblical parallelism, with the majority of references to biblical scholars, including Lowth. Although Lowth himself was conversant with discussions concerning the characteristics of classical Greek and Latin poetry, the effect of identifying parallelism as the primary feature of Hebrew poetry led him to avoid reflecting fully on Greek or English poetry, the theories associated with them, and how such literature or theories might illumine other features of Hebrew poetry.

In a related way, scholarly work on Hebrew poetry usually does not incorporate the broader discussions of poetry. With the recent exception of discussions that have utilized linguistics and poetics, this situation still obtains. One important goal of this book is to place the study of Hebrew poetry within the broader context of reflection about poetry, since Hebrew poets did have at their disposal diverse rhythmic patterns and various forms of parallelism as well as a whole series of other stylistic devices, the sorts of which appear prominently in poems composed in other languages.

THEORIES OF POETRY

Theories about poetry serve as maps. As with the science of cartography, diverse maps can be drawn. For example, any attempt to map the surface of the earth presents problems. Since the surface of a sphere cannot be replicated on a flat surface without distortion, cartographers have developed many ways of representing the earth on a flat surface. Some maps maintain more accurate dimensions, whereas other maps preserve directions more precisely. In many ways, maps are compromises. No one map can serve as an all-purpose guide. Rather, one must create maps that provide, as faithfully as possible, the desired projections that one wishes to convey. In the case of Hebrew poetry, we hope to provide a map that will do at least three things: (1) assist the reader to think about Hebrew poetry within the context of poetry composed in other languages; (2) place the discussion of Hebrew poetry within the context of recent technical work on Hebrew poetry during the last decade, in particular; and (3) alert readers of Hebrew poetry to its literary features, many of which have often gone unnoticed. We will address the first of these issues in this introduction, the second in the chapter on parallelism and the chapter on meter and rhythm, and the third in the chapter on poetic style.

Many questions are involved in the definition of poetry in any language. We will not be able to examine all of these, even some that are interesting, such as the arguments about whether the text itself or the reader is the ultimate source of a poem's meaning.[8] Instead, we will focus on the traditional issue regarding the distinction between poetry and other forms of linguistic expression. Discussion of this issue often centers on the distinction between art, belles lettres, of which poetry is one type, and other forms of expression. Within this nexus, the question of what makes poetry different from prose also arises.

We begin with the theories of poetry: What makes poetry poetic? Such theories tend to focus on a variety of issues. Some scholars have suggested that poetry is different from prose by dint of the peculiar set of grammatical rules that obtain in poetry when compared with those that undergird a language's prose. In the case of Hebrew poetry, one could say that a peculiar form of syntax, namely, parallelism, distinguishes poetry from prose. Others have maintained that the special features of poetry are not to be found so much in linguistic factors as in the composer's mind, psychological elements beyond language or, as some would say, poetic inspiration. Some who write on Hebrew poetry take this latter tack.

Those in the classical world of Plato and Aristotle debated about what such inspiration aroused. Inspiration was thought to provoke the "utterances of a madman" as well as to be a "divine release of the soul."[9] Some maintained that inspiration enabled imitation. Does poetry im-

7

itate reality? And what portion of reality—only the beautiful and not the ugly? Is poetry less or more concerned with truth than with history? Certainly within Hebrew Bible studies we hear the debates about how various historical narratives compare to the poetic expressions related to important events in Israel's history. The relationship of the poetic traditions of the wisdom literature and psalms continues to be discussed over against the literature that portrays in narrative prose "God's acts" in history. Which is better, the prose or the poetry? Does one more accurately portray what must have been the reality than the other? The question of what inspiration arouses among true and false prophets within Israel, while different from the classical Greek world's debate on inspiration, is a fight over what undeniably were opposing views of the world.

Even as we turn more specifically to several theories of poetry we should keep in view the larger context of such discussions. Definitions of poetry are not developed in isolation from our experience of language or from our other conceptualizing tasks. From antiquity to the present, theories of poetry have included philosophical and philological issues and have been influenced by the prevailing assumptions of both disciplines. There is no single, definitive map regarding theories of poetry. It is more important to understand the ways in which the poem, the poet, and the creative process are interrelated.

The expressive or emotive theory of poetry is familiar to most students of English literature. In the English language, this notion may be identified with Wordsworth's classic preface to the second edition of his *Lyrical Ballads*, but one may trace its roots to *On the Sublime*, which has been attributed to Longinus of the third century c.e. Such a view emphasizes that poetry is a form of discourse that expresses powerful or profound human emotions and feelings. By contrast, literature without such origins is prosaic and discursive, language of the mind but not of the heart. Robert Lowth's works have often been placed in this category, as has J.G. von Herder's two-volume study of Hebrew poetry. Herder maintained, regarding Hebrew poetry, that "a poetical image exists only in its connection with the emotion that prompted it."[10] Reading the commentary of James Muilenburg on Second Isaiah also gives one a sense of this emotive theory: "Isaiah 40–55 is a profoundly authentic product of the Hebraic mind and spirit. . . . The elevation of thought is matched by an intense lyricism."[11] Nonetheless, the work of most scholars on Hebrew poetry during the last decade is not guided by emotive theories.

8

Some who identify themselves as rhetorical critics, who focus on the self's (poet's) unique expression through imagination, metaphor, and intensity, seem as well to preserve this emotive theory.[12] The poet comes to the center. As Wordsworth indicated, he had "no right to the name of a Poet" unless he were to understand that "all good poetry is the spontaneous overflow of powerful feelings."[13] A section from Wordsworth's "Lucy" may serve to illustrate this theory. The speaker in the poem memorializes his now dead love. He never identifies the specific girl but allows the reader a glimpse of her significance through a piling up of metaphors. The halting rhythm in the next to the last line intensifies the finality of his loss.

> She dwelt among the untrodden ways
>   Beside the springs of Dove;
> A maid whom there were none to praise,
>   And very few to love.
>
> A violet by a mossy stone
>   Half-hidden from the eye!
> —Fair as a star, when only one
>   Is shining in the sky.
> She lived unknown, and few could know
>   When Lucy ceased to be;
> But she is in her grave, and, oh,
>   The difference to me!

This is not a poem that requires biographical or historical background or verifiability; in fact, no contemporary of Wordsworth or later critic has been able to identify the girl. The poem does not depend on narrative to express the emotion. Furthermore, as many recent critics have observed, such language stands in severe contrast to the referential quality of scientific language.

A theory such as this one, which focuses on the spontaneity of the poet, may seem more adequate to explain some kinds of Hebrew poetry than others. We should remember that theories, just as maps, serve diverse purposes. This particular theory reminds us of the emotive elements, which we must not forget even in the poetry that strikes any one individual reader as not particularly emotional. Moreover, this theory may also assist in the reading of Hebrew poetry, since it reminds the reader of the active role that individual poets—not just some impersonal setting in life—undoubtedly played in the composition of Hebrew poetry. We can lose sight of this expressive factor, given the anonymity of and our distance from this ancient poetry.

The mimetic or imitation of reality theory provides a second perspective. Both Plato and Aristotle thought of poetry as an imitation of human activities, even though their philosophical presuppositions provided different understandings of the object for and the means of mimesis. Whether realist or idealist, the mimetic theory highlights the poem, not the poet. The poem is the copy, the mirror, the representation. Therefore this theory focuses on the relationship between poem (imitation) and the world (that which is imitated). How well the image represents the reality becomes the mode of valuation, whether the representation is of a transcendent reality or a mundane beauty.

Some have thought that such mimesis is the essence of art. On the one hand, this could be thought of negatively as a kind of third-rate imitation that must be judged alongside all other endeavors. On the other hand, the peculiarity of the representation could be thought of as a unique opportunity to gain access to realities unattainable by law or politics or any other human activity. For example, proponents of this theory would maintain that history could not provide the same access to the deeper, more profound imitations of events expressed in poetry. Poetic mirrors permit a creative and provocative glimpse of reality not found in other forms of expression.

Shelley's A *Defense of Poetry* attests to one dimension of this incomparable quality that the poem embodies. In the first quarter of the eighteenth century, he wrote a response to an attack on poetry in which someone claimed that "in whatever degree poetry is cultivated, it must necessarily be to the neglect of some branch of useful study."[14] Shelley countered:

> All high poetry is infinite; it is as the first acorn, which contained all oaks potentially. . . . A great poem is a fountain for ever overflowing with the waters of wisdom and delight. . . . The most glorious poetry that has ever been communicated to the world is probably but a shadow of the original conceptions of the poet. . . . Poetry turns all things to loveliness.[15]

This stance suggests that all great poetry provides not only an imitation of but even our only access to the world's values and order.

The title of chapter 4 in Robert Alter's *The Art of Biblical Poetry*, "Truth and Poetry in the Book of Job," appears to be an excellent contemporary example of the mimetic theory. When discussing the divine discourses at the end of Job, he refers to them as a "revelation." Then he maintains, "Through this pushing of poetic expression toward its own upper limits, the concluding speech helps us see the panorama of creation, as perhaps we could do only through poetry, with the eyes of God."[16] We should be cautious not to label Alter as one who uses this theory exclusively throughout his book, but here it is evident.

Third, goal-oriented theories move beyond imitation to focus on the rhetorical effect of a poem's persuasion and on the end to which a poem is directed. Here, neither the poem nor the poet is the primary focus; rather, the audience assumes center stage. Good poetry is a crafted product that evokes pleasure in or affects significantly the reader. Poetry is thought of as a crafted product of the poet. One can discern this theory at work in the statement of Shelley quoted above when he suggests that poetry turns "all things to loveliness." While the focus is on the effect brought on the reader, the poem itself was usually thought to be an object that was crafted according to a very specific set of rules. Thus, if the rules were followed, good poetry would result and the proper ends would be evoked in the reader.

Much of the last decade's work on Hebrew poetry has examined the poet's craft. However, attention has not been directed to what the crafted object achieves. Rather, the search for the "basic unit" of Hebrew verse has clearly involved the search for the craft's governing rules. Among the recent works, Michael O'Connor's has been criticized for its preoccupation with mechanics.[17] James Kugel has been faulted for ignoring larger units, focusing only on "seconding" within "parallel lines" and being unaware of how the larger units—poems—function.[18] Adele Berlin may best represent, in a positive sense, this pragmatic theory. She says that the value of studying biblical parallelism is not only to understand better the "elasticity" of parallelism but also to provide "our entrée into the message."[19] "Parallelism, like other formal features in a text, *does* help to structure the text and thereby has an impact on how its meaning is arrived at."[20]

Finally, there are two theoretical perspectives that may be considered together. One has been referred to as the "objective theory,"[21] which suggests that a poem is an object unto itself, not an imitation of any other reality. The other might be referred to as the indeterminacy theory, which may be associated with deconstructionist critics.[22] These theories belong together for two reasons. First, both represent important positions in the late twentieth century while at the same time having foundations in the classical discussions. Second, and more important, both of these theories focus in a radical way on the poem itself and on the ways of reading that poem.

These two theories stress the power of art for art's sake. Both understand the poem as a self-contained, new reality with indeterminate, even conflicting, power for the reader. The reader may be understood as the poet. The one who reads also writes or constructs the text. Or the poet can be understood as an invisible creator, not imitating a reality somewhere out there but genuinely constructing a reality all its own. The poem is neither an imitation of another reality, a sponta neous expression, nor the result of manipulating some external elements. The poet is not a strategist who has mastered some rhetorical rules nor an instrumentality through whom words are transmitted nor an observer with special, acute sensitivities. The reader is not a passive receiver, not one looking at a poem as though it were a mirror of some reality, not one who might be persuaded by some set of external values crafted in the poem.

This theoretical position may seem ambiguous and even self-contradictory. According to the words of one interpreter, this should not be surprising, because "self-contradiction . . . is the very language of poetry, and the theory of poetry . . . must itself *be* poetry."[23] This viewpoint has led some to despair of ever understanding a poem. Others have taken up the ambiguity as a signal of language's metaphorical multiplicity, of the expansiveness of texts, and ultimately of the playfulness of words.

Few scholars interested in classical Hebrew poetry have taken up the radical dimensions of these ideas. It is interesting that several contemporary literary theorists have worked, using rabbinic traditions of interpretation, to develop their theories.[24] They have found warrants for the multivalence of texts, the play between poem and commentary, and the uneasy yet necessary balance between understanding and misunderstanding. Whether we opt for the more or the less radical of these ideas, we, as readers of poetry—literature that evokes strong responses—find ourselves involved in intense readings as well as intense discussions of its essential features. We need not think that the "meaning of a poem can only be another poem," but surely the reading of a poem may become a powerful component of the realities we experience and create.

It might appear that the seemingly unmanageable array of poetic theories illustrates the futility of such theorizing. In contrast, we think an awareness of these diverse theories serves readers and interpreters by "establishing a point of vantage" that may yield "distinctive insights into the properties and relations of poems."[25] Consequently, it is important to consider four points of vantage as we turn either to the Hebrew poetry itself or to the literature about it:

1. The interrelationships of poet and poem.
2. The expression of either direct or indirect value.
3. The glimpse, sometimes given in the poem, of the process that called forth the poem.
4. The role of the reader.

We do not assume here a single theory of poetry, nor will we offer a conclusive definition of poetry or even of Hebrew poetry. Rather, we will offer ways to understand the poetry in the Hebrew Bible. Some suggest that naming a piece of literature a poem is to attribute value and importance to it. Robert Frost once said, "'Poet' is a praise-word." The Hebrew poets do not tell us that they have written a poem. They write in verse and it is our task, as both readers and interpreters, to determine whether a text is a poem and how that determination assists our reading.

POETRY-PROSE CONTINUUM

We return to the question of how to distinguish poetry from prose, since in the last decade this query has become a central issue within the study of Hebrew poetry. Kugel argues that the distinction is best understood as involving different points on a continuum, namely, that there is no sharp dividing line between poetry and prose. On another side is Alter, who maintains that Hebrew prose is a natural expression of ancient Semitic culture, whereas Hebrew poetry is related to the ethical monotheism unique to the religion of ancient Israel.[26] For him, there is a fundamental conceptual distinction between prose and poetry. Alter does maintain, however, that there are two primary generative forces in Hebrew poetry: intensification (parallelism) and narrativity. Since narrativity is important to prose composition as well, Alter's judgment, too, seems, finally, to blur the distinction between prose and poetry.

Without presenting the conclusions of this volume before the analysis and argument that lead up to them, it seems important to foreshadow the basic position that we will be advocating. There is literature that may reasonably be construed as poetry in the Hebrew Bible.

13

This literature shares fundamental affinities with poetic literature outside the Bible, and not just poetic texts from the ancient Near East. As a result, we reject the notion that there is no poetry in the Hebrew Bible. This judgment is not intended to deny that Hebrew prose and poetic literature share important features. Nonetheless, the distinction between poetry and prose is not an imposition of foreign Greek categories on Hebrew.[27] Rather, in Hebrew as with many other languages there is a body of literature that may reasonably be identified as poetry.

The three basic categories that we use to discuss Hebrew poetry—parallelism, rhythm, and style—are important for the discussion of all literature. Parallelism of various sorts occurs in prose as well as in poetry. Rhythm, which is basic to all human speech, is important in prose as well as in poetry. And figures of speech, for example, metaphor or personification, appear prominently in prose as well as poetic texts. As a result, we may reject various and competing claims that either parallelism (so Lowth) or meter (so Freedman) serves as *the* hallmark of Hebrew poetry. Instead, we maintain that all three of these features occur prominently in poetry, though in a more intense, denser, or more compact way than they do in prose. Neither rhythm/meter, parallelism, nor other poetic techniques can, in and of themselves, serve as a hallmark for identifying poetic expression. Poetic expression constitutes a subtle interplay of the rhythmic expression of carefully crafted human speech wrought with special attention to artistic effect. Hebrew poetry constitutes these features along with a perceptible, elastic parallelism.

THREE APPROACHES

Study of Hebrew poetry today is indebted to generations of scholars who have analyzed the corpus of biblical and nonbiblical Hebrew poetry. Since the perceptions, vocabulary, methods, and conclusions of these thinkers have so significantly colored the way we now think about Hebrew poetry, attention to some key figures is important as we move toward new ways of thinking about and understanding this poetry. Given the scope of this volume, it is not possible to survey all those who have contributed to our understanding of Hebrew poetry. Throughout the discussion, however, we hope to highlight those figures who have been most influential in the history of reflection about this ancient Semitic poetry, including both authors from antiquity, such as Philo, and more recent writers, such as Lowth, Herder, and Gray.

The last several decades have seen the appearance of numerous important studies, many of which advocate a fundamental rethinking of classical Hebrew poetry. Such recent work on Hebrew poetry has proceeded on at least three tracks: technical studies of Hebrew prosody (which, despite the strict sense of prosody, have often involved considerably more than attention to metrics and versification), concern for reading and understanding the Bible as literature, and the practical work of interpretation of the biblical text involving, as that study often does, standard historical-critical methods (e.g., form criticism and redaction criticism).[28]

The first of these concerns, prosodic analysis of Hebrew poetry, has, particularly in North America, been associated with the work of Frank Moore Cross, David Noel Freedman, and their students.[29] As Cross and Freedman explain, their style of analyzing Hebrew poetry stands in the tradition of metric analysis, particularly that of Julius Ley, Eduard Sievers, and W. F. Albright.[30] It was, however, the impulse of epigraphic discoveries—ancient texts written in the original script and orthography and composed in languages that were very similar to ancient Hebrew, for example, Ugaritic—that provided the impetus for prosodic analysis in the mid-twentieth century.[31] By assessing what they took to be the earliest exemplars of Hebrew poetry and by comparing that canon to the extrabiblical texts, Cross and Freedman thought it possible to discover the prosodic, that is, metrical, structure of ancient Hebrew poetry (see p. 40 below). Others, such as Terence Collins and Michael O'Connor, have examined Hebrew poetry in an attempt either to discern its essential features or to examine how it works grammatically. Valuable as much of this work is, it often stops short of the larger interpretive task, namely, discussing poetics or poetry.[32] Furthermore, because some recent work has been extremely technical in character, those involved in the literary study of the Bible or more general interpretive efforts have not availed themselves of the resources that these technical works provide.

The other two approaches are quite different. One is a relative newcomer to the study of the Bible—the Bible as literature movement—whereas the other constitutes a long-standing tradition in both Christian and Jewish circles, namely, the learned interpretation of canonical literature. The former approach, reading the Bible as literature, has recently flourished in a variety of journals, monograph series, and individual books. David Robertson's *The Old Testament and the Literary Critic*, published in this series (GBS.OTS), is one example of this way of reading biblical literature, as is Alter's more recent *The Art of Biblical Poetry*. The obvious goal of scholars who advocate this approach is to read biblical prose and poetry in ways not fundamentally different from the ways they read Milton, Dickens, Eliot, or Frost. The interpretive categories are those of the literary critic, for example, the analysis of characterization, plot, theme, motif, symbolism, and the like. Our volume depends, in some ways, on the results of this approach.

The latter perspective, that of the learned interpretation of biblical literature, is one that has often stood in the service of religious communities. Calvin's and Luther's Old Testament commentaries were designed, essentially, to serve the interests of their respective churches. Even today, when commentaries are written for a scholarly audience, they are often published by church-related publishing houses, for example, the Hermeneia series of Fortress Press or the Interpretation series of John Knox Press. The authors of such commentaries, whether ancient or modern, were interested in explicating the meaning(s) of the text by utilizing whatever perspectives—allegorical, philological, historical-critical, or theological—they deemed appropriate. In these commentaries, authors working on Old Testament poetic texts have been forced to reckon with the problems of Hebrew poetry. As a result, it is not unusual to find an excursus or a special chapter devoted to the Hebrew poetry of Psalms or of one of the prophets. Sometimes these treatments have offered insights beyond the scope of the specific biblical literature under examination. However, and this is as true for modern as it is for ancient commentaries, they have often not been in dialogue with recent developments in the study of Hebrew poetry.

These three approaches—analysis of Hebrew poetry, reading Hebrew Bible poetry as literature, and interpretive work generally—deserve to stand in dialogue so that they may mutually enhance the goal of reading the biblical literature with understanding and appreciation.

RELATIONSHIP OF METHODS

One final question deserves a response: What is the relationship between the study of Hebrew poetry and other ways of examining biblical texts? It is commonplace for grammatical and prosodic study of poetic texts to operate in something of a vacuum. Along with text-critical study, these perspectives are traditionally termed "lower criticism." They have in common an interest in establishing and translating the text. However, questions about the date of composition, authorship, editing of the text, as well as its overall meaning, are not typically addressed from these perspectives. Rather, source criticism, form criticism, tradition history, redaction criticism, and the general application of the historical-critical method (the so-called higher-critical perspectives) have proved useful for addressing these concerns.[33] Ideally the interpreter will use various perspectives, both philological and historical-critical, in order to formulate the interpretation of a biblical text. To be sure, scholars sometimes use one or another of these methods in isolation from other perspectives. However, scholars, whether in commentaries or other interpretive pieces, are obliged to demonstrate how the discrete perspectives may be integrated within the larger interpretive task.

Recent technical work on Hebrew poetry has not been integrated into commentaries and more general interpretive publications—with some exceptions, such as Patrick Miller's *Interpreting the Psalms*. The work of O'Connor and Collins, to cite obvious examples, is so fully devoted to the grammar and syntax of Hebrew poetry, and so technical in its presentation, that the task of integrating their work with other interpretive perspectives, which the authors themselves do not pretend to attempt, remains for others to accomplish. To date, this has not occurred.[34] Cataloging poetic lines by grammatical type, though an important exercise, is not identical with understanding the meanings of a poem.

In addition, there are important reasons for the study of Hebrew poetry to be held in dialogue with diverse methodological perspectives. Textual criticism may serve as an example. References to the term *metri causa* illustrate the point we make. This phrase, often used by text critics, refers to a judgment, *causa*, based on an understanding of Hebrew meter, *metri*. The judgment typically involves the proposed addition or deletion of a Hebrew word from the text. The scholar thinks the word or phrase in question either is necessary for, in the case of addition, or disturbs, in the case of deletion, the meter presumed in that text. To make matters especially difficult, such *metri causa* proposals frequently are presented without the support of ancient manuscripts. The metric disturbance to which they refer generally is presumed to have occurred before variant manuscript traditions developed. So, for example, one may refer to an influential study of

Israelite religion that includes metric analysis of Hebrew poetic texts, that of Frank Moore Cross, *Canaanite Myth and Hebrew Epic.*[35] In that volume, Cross reconstructs a number of such texts as they may have occurred in their pristine form. In this regard, *metri causa* arguments occur with some regularity. For example, when working on Judg. 5:23, Cross argues that the first poetic line should be translated "Curse ye Meroz, saith Yahweh."[36] Most modern translations read something similar to NRSV, namely, "Curse Meroz, says the angel of the LORD." The word that NRSV translates as "angel" (one could also translate "messenger") did not, in Cross's judgment, occur in the original text: "We have omitted *malʾāk* as secondary for metrical reasons." This is a classic *metri causa* argument. There are no ancient manuscripts that support the judgment. Rather, the argument rests solely on a decision based on the metric regularity presumed to exist in the verse.[37] In our judgment, such decisions are risky indeed, though to be sure sometimes necessary, because they presume so much about something about which we know so little, namely, meter in classical Hebrew poetry.

In a similar vein, recent literary-critical study of Hebrew poetry has not regularly been integrated either with lower- or higher-critical perspectives. In fact, one senses a certain iconoclasm on the part of some literary critics, namely, that higher-critical concerns are of minimal value and that the literature may be comprehended without attention to the date of composition or the origins or development of a particular text. Alter's work on prophetic poetry may serve as an example. When attempting to define the salient features of this type of Hebrew poetry, he treats several examples of poetry found in Isaiah. His argument involves what he perceives as a tendency for prophetic poetry "to lift the utterances to a second power of signification, aligning statements that are addressed to a concrete historical situation with an archetypal horizon."[38] Such poetry, Alter suggests, tends to place historical events within a cosmic perspective; history is viewed from an almost mythological vantage point. As a way of developing this position, he cites Isa. 14:4-21; 5:26-30; and 24:17-20. After commenting on the last of these texts, he states: "But whatever Isaiah may have had in mind historically, it is clear that the sweep of his poetic language has become properly mythological, catching up in its movement the beginning and end of all things."[39] Such a claim presents serious problems to the student of Israelite prophecy, to the student of apocalypticism, and to the person who specializes in the study of Isaiah. The reason is quite simple.

18

Most scholars who have worked on the Book of Isaiah, particularly on Isaiah 24–27, regard these chapters as an exilic or postexilic supplement to the preexilic literature that may properly be attributed to Isaiah of Jerusalem. Isaiah 24–27 is often called "the Isaianic Apocalypse," a label that highlights its almost apocalyptic character and that serves to distinguish those four chapters from other material in First Isaiah.[40] It is the case that deutero-prophetic literature such as the Isaianic Apocalypse does tend to present Israelite religion in an almost mythic vein, in a way removed from the world of mundane reality. This perspective, however, is really a step beyond that of classical Israelite prophecy, and not necessarily typical of it. As a result, Alter's judgments about prophetic poetry, based in part on his inclusion of Isa. 24:17-20 in an assessment of Isaiah and, more generally, Israelite prophecy, are skewed because his work does not take into account other scholarship on the literature that he examined. Although he draws "historical" conclusions about the prophet, he has not relied on the results of historical scholarship. Thus it is difficult to integrate his judgments about the Book of Isaiah and about prophetic poetry into other discussions concerning these topics. Such an approach places literary considerations in unfortunate isolation from other ways of analyzing biblical literature. One of our goals is to demonstrate how such literary considerations can be related to broader scholarly discussions.

2
Parallelism

Anyone who interprets Hebrew poetry must understand parallelism. This has been the case since the mid-eighteenth century, when Robert Lowth presented his lectures on the subject. Terms such as synonymous, antithetic, and synthetic parallelism are common in introductions to Hebrew poetry written after the time of Lowth. They continue to be used but with some significant variations in meaning from what Lowth intended.

The language of parallelism doubtless will continue. However, the major thrust of the last decade has involved the development of better theoretical models for conceptualizing parallelism. Moreover, scholars have provided detailed poetic analyses of selected Hebrew texts using these new models. Before we summarize the most prominent of these recent developments in the analysis of parallelism, it is necessary to understand the seminal contributions of Lowth.

ROBERT LOWTH

Robert Lowth's lectures marked a major advance in understanding "the Sacred Poetry of the Hebrews," and they remain seminal in virtually every discussion of Hebrew poetry. Nearly two hundred and fifty years after he wrote his lectures, one finds reference to them in scholarly monographs, in detailed articles reporting research on the most technical aspects of parallelism, and in introductions to the characteristics of Hebrew poetry. Lowth argued that the dominant feature of that literature "consists chiefly in a certain quality, resemblance, or parallelism, between the members of each period; so that in two lines (or members of the same period) things for the most part shall answer to things, and words to words, as if fitted to each other by a kind of

21

rule or measure."[1] For Lowth, parallelism was the hallmark of Hebrew poetry.

In order to appreciate fully the significance of Lowth's lectures, it is important to identify three simple factors that have often been forgotten. First, he was participating in a long-standing debate regarding the relationship of poetry and prophecy as well as a discussion of the origins and purpose of poetry. Put another way, his assessment of Hebrew poetry involved other important topics in Hebrew Bible studies, especially the nature of prophetic literature, which he maintained was poetry, as were the psalms. He had not set out to revolutionize the understanding of Hebrew poetry.

Second, following Lowth's two introductory lectures comes what, in the English edition, is called the "first part," a lecture on meter. This section recognizes the problems of attempting to discern meter in Hebrew poetry. In the published edition of the lectures, there is an appendix disproving Bishop Hare's metrical system known to Lowth's audience. Lowth's own views on meter seem not altogether clear, as is exemplified by his observation that within the parallelism one "apprehends a considerable part of the Hebrew metre."[2] It would appear that, for Lowth, meter and parallelism were integrally related. Since he focused on the line (and the relationship of lines to each other) and since much of Hebrew poetry yields lines of reasonably regular length, it is not surprising that he suggested relationships between parallelism and meter.

Third, it is only in the third part of his tome,[3] on the "specific species" of Hebrew poetry, that Lowth develops the notion of parallelism. In lecture 19, which is part of his discussion of prophetic poetry, he discusses synonymous, antithetic, and synthetic (or constructive) parallelism.

Lowth's division of parallelism into three basic types remains dominant in virtually every introductory discussion of Hebrew poetry published through the 1980s.[4] Of these three types, synthetic parallelism had, until the last decade, received the most attention. Discussion of synthetic parallelism usually amounted to a series of refined distinctions to explain the diverse ways the parallel lines were really not "true" parallelism.[5] The author of one helpful description of Hebrew poetry suggested that his own work was merely an "elaboration and enrichment of Lowth's viewpoint."[6] As we will see, this situation has changed substantively in the last decade.

BASIC NOMENCLATURE

The nomenclature used in the discussion of Hebrew poetry has been less consistent than the fundamental concept of parallelism. Scholars have used diverse terms (e.g., stich, line, hemistich, verset, colon) to name the two entities that correspond with each other to constitute the parallelism. Throughout this work we will refer to each constituent part of the parallelism as a colon or line. A relationship of various sorts, grammatic or semantic, between lines constitutes parallelism.

Even the concept of the line in Hebrew poetry has become the focus of debate.[7] Some contemporary analysts use "line" to refer to bicolon or tricolon (Alter, Collins, Kugel, and Pardee), while our practice follows that of Berlin, Geller, O'Connor, and Watson. Part of the debate has hinged on whether or not one was identifying the line through an identification of stress. It is generally agreed, however, that the colon is the basic unit (not the bicolon) and that it most frequently occurs together with one or two other cola.[8]

The delineation of lines often presents problems. That is, it is not always obvious where a colon begins and ends, since few ancient Hebrew manuscripts have set out Hebrew poetry in the lineation of our modern critical texts or translations. There is additional terminological variation beyond that associated with the use of line. Some will use the term "verse" to refer to the basic unit, whether a single colon or more. We will generally avoid the term "verse." In fact, we will contend that there is no basic or fundamental Hebrew poetic unit other than the line. It seems to us more helpful to distinguish the separate cola in whatever combination they occur rather than to assume any basic or ideal combination, such as the bicolon.

The bicolon, or two-colon unit, occurs most frequently. It is sometimes called a couplet or line-pair. While this is the most typical combination in Hebrew poetry, there are other units. Monocola even exist—for example, Ps. 1:1. The presence of monocola suggests that parallelism is not the only factor in the creation of Hebrew poetry. While a monocolon does not have a direct relationship to another line, it does provide variation to other units—for example, a bicolon—and thus creates contrast with the more frequent parallelistic structures.

Before we turn to the bicolon, a word about other combinations is important. The tricolon, a combination of three cola, appears frequently enough that all readers should anticipate finding this three-line unit in Hebrew poetry. A tricolon appears in the familiar opening to Psalm 100.

> Make a joyful noise to the LORD, all the earth.
> Worship the LORD with gladness;
> come into his presence with singing.

Although some have suggested that the bicolon is the basic unit, even when considering a tricolon, this contention is problematic. Stephen Geller understands the tricolon as a sequence of interrelated bicola (A + B and B + C) or three lines understood as a monocolon plus bicolon.[9] However, the example from Psalm 100 illustrates a parallelism that surely is best understood as A / A'/ A" (cf. Hos. 5:1). There are other significant examples where both semantic and grammatic reasons support three parallel lines (cf. in the examples the discussion of Ps. 1:1, p. 93 below).

The consensus among scholars is that there are indeed multi-colon units even beyond the tricolon. Watson[10] provides examples of some of these combinations of cola beyond the tricolon. In some cases one could contend that instead of a tetracolon (or, as Watson calls it, a quatrain), one has either two bicola or even a tricolon plus a monocolon. However, when semantic and grammatic reasons are introduced into the discussion, there is no reason in principle that should preclude finding various multi-colon combinations.

The bicolon (more than one bicolon = bicola) is the most frequently occurring combination, for example,

> It is good to give thanks, O LORD,
> to sing praises to your name, O Most High.
> Ps. 92:1

A short pause is implied at the end of "LORD" and a longer pause after "Most High." This can be graphically represented in the following manner: _____ / _____ //. The single slash indicates the short pause and the double slash indicates the longer pause.

SYNONYMOUS, ANTITHETIC, SYNTHETIC PARALLELISM

We turn now to Lowth's description of parallelism. Both citations from Psalms in the previous section exemplify what Lowth would have called synonymous parallelism. He considered this "species" of parallelism the most sublime.[11] It "consists chiefly in a certain equality, resemblance, or parallelism" where "the same sentiment is repeated in different, but equivalent terms."[12]

By way of contrast, antithetic parallelism "is not confined to any particular form; for sentiments are opposed to sentiments, words to words, singulars to singulars, plurals to plurals."[13] Lowth takes examples from Prov. 27:6-7, which includes two antithetical bicola. The "but" reinforces the semantic antithesis for the English reader.

> The blows of a friend are faithful;
> But the kisses of an enemy are treacherous.
> The cloyed will trample upon a honey-comb;
> But to the hungry every bitter thing is sweet.[14]

The concluding bicolon of Psalm 1 in our examples also illustrates what Lowth would have called antithetic parallelism.

> For the LORD knows the way of the righteous,
> but the way of the wicked will perish.

Lowth calls the third "species" of parallelism "synthetic." He defines it as syntax in which "sentences answer to each other, not by the iteration of the same image or sentiment, or the opposition of their contraries, but merely by the form of construction."[15] Lowth recognized that cola could be related even if there was no semantic parallelism. He offered Hos. 14:5-6 (Heb., 14:6-7) as an example:

> I will be as dew to Israel:
> He shall blossom as the lily;
> And he shall strike his roots like Lebanon:
> His suckers shall spread,
> And his glory shall be as the olive-tree,
> And his smell as Lebanon.

In these verses there is neither apparent semantic synonymity nor antithesis; rather, in Hebrew the lines are of similar length and involve other kinds of semantic development, and grammatical devices that enforce parallelism, for example, simile. Furthermore, Lowth and his followers have used the repeated bicolon in Amos 1 and 2 to illustrate synthetic parallelism that involved repetition but no antithesis or synonymity.

For three transgressions of . . . . ,
and for four, I will not revoke the punishment . . .

Lowth's recognition that parallelism went beyond the semantic levels presaged the developments that have emerged in the last decade.

There was, however, a problem with the variety of constructions designated as synthetic parallelism as well as the more general issue of what was to be regarded as the basic features of parallelism. As a result, Lowth may be credited with much of the confusion that derives from the term "synthetic parallelism." He suggested that synthetic parallelism occurs where neither semantic antithesis nor synonymity exists but where there are formal ties (grammatical and metrical) between cola. Unfortunately he neglected to distinguish adequately a series of issues that certainly should be clear by now, even if they were not when George Gray wrote his major critique of Lowth's synthetic parallelism over sixty years ago.[16] Synthetic parallelism[17] had become a summary category for everything in Hebrew poetry that did not belong to synonymous or antithetic parallelism. Lowth's third type of parallelism did seem necessary, since it is clear that varieties of parallelism beyond semantic antithesis and synonymity exist. Both Lowth's awareness of this fact and the subsequent attempts to develop the category of synthetic parallelism are major factors that have generated much of the last decade's work on parallelism.

Lowth's lectures gave a broad definition of parallelism, but the definition lacked precision. He did not have at his disposal the linguistic tools that would have enabled him to articulate carefully the interrelationship of semantic parallelism with other types of parallelism. He could identify the three types of parallelism within a single text because he understood that at the root of parallelism was the idea of correspondence. His categories permitted him to identify the mingling of diverse parallelism within a single text. Psalm 14:1-2 illustrates the shifting from one type of parallelism to another. The bicola, according to a Lowthian perspective,[18] shift from synthetic to synonymous:

Fools say in their hearts,	
"There is no God."	*synthetic*
They are corrupt, they do abominable deeds,	
there is no one who does good.	*synonymous*
The LORD looks down from heaven	
on humankind,	*synthetic*
to see if there are any who are wise,	
who seek after God.	*synonymous*

26

Use of these identifications does not allow one to identify grammatic elements that are clear in the Hebrew text, for example, contrasting verbal and nonverbal cola. They do not enable the reader to see the relationships between the repeated "there is no . . . " (*'ên*) in the first synthetic and synonymous bicola or the repetition of God (*'ĕlōhîm*) in the first and last bicola. More important, these Lowthian categories do not assist the interpreter in establishing from the beginning of this psalm its major semantic antithesis between the fool and the deity.

NEW UNDERSTANDINGS

The term "parallelism" continues to be used to describe the relationship between cola. New terms such as "matching," "intensifying," and "seconding" have emerged to clarify the kind of correspondence meant by parallelism. New concepts, largely derived from linguistics, have enabled us to move beyond Lowth's categories in fundamental ways. The first such development is the fact that we can no longer equate parallelism and Hebrew poetry. The second development consists of drawing our attention from the poetic line to the "unit of sense." This entails both greater attention to individual words, sounds, and forms, as well as to the connections between these elements. After looking at these developments, we will elaborate some of the different aspects[19] of parallelism, namely, grammatic and semantic parallelism.

First, until the last decade few would have questioned the equation: Parallelism equals poetry in Hebrew. Lowth may have implied that parallelism existed in prose as well as in poetry, but the dominant thrust of his work suggests that where parallelism is found, there is Hebrew poetry. However, Kugel has pointed out that Hebrew prose yields a variety of features that may be termed parallelism. For example, one may examine the following prose from Genesis 22. When it is set out on the page as poetry, one can readily observe the correspondence between lines.

> I will indeed bless you,
> and I will make your offspring as numerous
> as the stars of heaven
> and as the sand that is on the seashore.

Gen. 22:17

In addition, Kugel displays Num. 5:12-15 in parallel lines.[20] In fact, as he notes, there are parallel structures in every telephone book in the

world! Lists provide excellent examples of lines that may be understood as parallel.[21] Some lists indeed function in poetic texts to further
the poetic effect (Ps. 148:7-13), but not all lists are poetry.

Moreover, Kugel observed that some poetic texts include lines that
are difficult to identify as parallel on almost any grounds. Psalm 119:54
presents two lines that can hardly be designated parallel: "Your laws
were my songs/ in my dwelling place//" (Kugel's translation). It has
been argued in a study of early Hebrew poetry that 12 percent of the
corpus exhibits nonparallel lines.[22] In sum, an easy equation between
poetry and parallelism is no longer possible.

Most contemporary interpreters of Hebrew literature agree that poetry and prose are on a continuum. However, contending that poetry
and prose are best understood on a continuum is not to suggest that
we must abandon the distinction between poetry and prose.[23] There
are pieces of Hebrew literature—some refer to texts like Genesis 22—
that use parallelism and are terse or even paratactic—qualities often
associated with poetry. But no one would contend that Genesis 22, the
"binding of Isaac," is poetry. A reader's identification of a text as poetry
is determined by a variety of complex factors. It would take us much
too far afield to review the diverse perspectives surrounding this notion of a poetry-prose continuum. It is important to discard our often
simplistic ideas of the distinctions between poetry and prose when
coming to Hebrew poetry, whether the distinctions are between parallelism and no parallelism, "high" and "low" style, or rhyme and no
rhyme.[24]

As indicated in chapter 1, most readers rely on the format of the
printed page, whether looking at the standard critical edition of the
Hebrew text or at some English translation, to determine whether a
text is prose or poetry. A prose text is printed from margin to margin,
whereas poetic texts are indented so as to "look" poetic.[25] Such
formatting makes the distinction between poetry and prose for most
readers.

Although we will not attempt to make the case that any one particular text is or is not poetry, we must not ignore the issue, particularly
as regards its importance for the assessment of a text's meaning. Said
another way, "Poetry and interpretation are not matters that should be
dealt with separately; rather, a deeper sensitivity to the poetic character of a text can enhance our understanding, and attention to poetic
features may aid the interpretive process and its results."[26]

If parallelism is not coextensive with poetry in some straightforward way, and if parallelism involves more than semantic synonymity and antithesis, then some new conceptual scheme is necessary. For some, the study of linguistics provides the basis for a new approach, one that moves beyond the poetic line to words, grammar, sounds, and syntax. As Berlin has said, "Linguistics is fast becoming the prism through which poetry is viewed."[27] She correctly observes, however, that "if the grammatical aspect provides the skeleton of the parallelism then the lexical and semantic aspects are its flesh and blood."[28] Linguistics has assisted our precision in identifying the panoply of elements enriching parallelism, but not at the expense of ignoring semantics.

Linguistics includes the study of language, the principles of its organization, and the exploration of theoretical understandings. Since language is the medium of poetry, it seems appropriate that linguistics has become central to the interpretation of poems. This does not mean that extralinguistic factors are insignificant in the writing of or the interpreting of poetry. We saw in chapter 1 that there are various theories of poetry which, indeed, extend the understanding of a poem beyond a purely linguistic phenomenon.[29]

It has been said that the single poetic line is a "unit of attention" but not necessarily a "unit of sense."[30] Those discussing Hebrew poetry, while certainly interested in the line, have turned to the diverse elements that make up both units of attention and units of sense. The fact that parallelism is so central to Hebrew poetry demands attention to the word as well as to the way words are linked. Attention to these matters is accomplished through turning to what may be termed grammatic and semantic parallelism.

Recent scholarly work on Hebrew poetry has advanced our understandings of grammatic parallelism.[31] These studies have identified syntactic, morphologic, and phonetic forms of parallelism. One of the earliest studies of the last decade, O'Connor's, examined word order (syntax) in each poetic unit. With diverse nomenclature the constituent parts in each colon—subject, verb, object, and modifiers—were identified. Isa. 9:6 (Heb., v. 5) illustrates a bicolon where each colon includes a subject, a verb, and a modifier:

> For a child has been born for us,
>   a son given to us;

On many occasions the grammatic parallelism coincides with the meaning or semantic parallelism, as in the Isaiah example. Child and

29

son are synonymous terms, the verbs convey a sense of equivalence, and the prepositional phrase is identical. Repetitive parallelism, such as the prepositional phrase "to us," should not be neglected. Even when repeated at some distance, repetitive parallelism brings together every level of equivalence—semantic as well as several levels of grammatic parallelism (morphologic, syntactic, and phonetic).[32]

However, the relationship of semantic and grammatic parallelism is not always immediately apparent. Observe Ps. 111:5 (Berlin's translation):

> Food he gives to his fearers;
> He remembers his covenant forever.

In both cola, the word order, although slightly different in the Hebrew, includes a subject, a verb, an object, and a modifier. The semantic parallelism, despite grammatic equivalence, is not transparent. Can remembering a covenant and giving food be understood as identical or similar activities? The grammatic parallelism enforces the correspondence between the lines. But what of the meaning?

Berlin provides an answer that derives from linguistics. She has borrowed from linguistic studies the notions of paradigmatic and syntagmatic relationships.[33] If one understands the relationship between lines or phrases as one in which the thought expressed in the first colon continues into the second colon, one may speak of a syntagmatic relationship. On the other hand, if one understands the relationship between lines or phrases as one in which the thought expressed in the one colon substitutes for a line or phrase in another colon, then we understand a paradigmatic relationship. Syntagmatic relationships continue or advance the relationship. Paradigmatic relationships substitute. Her translation of Isa. 40:9 serves as a good illustration of both.

> Ascend a high hill, herald to Zion;
> Lift your voice aloud, herald to Jerusalem!

One ascends the hill and then the voice is lifted. There is a continuation, a sequence of action. One can then say that the relationship of the actions in the bicolon is syntagmatic. On the other hand, the herald to Jerusalem substitutes in the second colon for the herald to Zion in the first colon. These are certainly meant to refer to the same individual. In other words, it is not one herald going up the hill and another lifting a voice, since Zion and Jerusalem are identical entities. The one substitutes for the other. We can say, then, that the addressees in this bicolon function paradigmatically.

To return to Ps. 111:5, the grammatic parallelism assisted us in seeing the correspondence through the essentially equivalent syntax in each colon. At the semantic level the correspondence is not transparent, because the relationship between giving food and remembering a covenant are not synonymous, nor are they antithetical. If we consider the paradigmatic and syntagmatic relationships, however, we gain new perspectives. The notion of giving food to those in a relationship with the LORD (the ones fearing God) may be easily extended by the expression of the remembering of a relationship, namely, the covenant. The interpreter is reminded of the covenant meal in Exod. 24:11 at which Moses and the chief people of Israel "ate and drank" with God.

GRAMMATIC, MORPHOLOGIC, SEMANTIC PARALLELISM

Grammatic parallelism may function at any of the diverse levels of language. In the current discussions of Hebrew poetry, there are different ways of distinguishing the parallelism we have chosen to group under the category of grammatic. Some will separate grammatic from phonetic (or phonologic) elements, even going so far as to understand sound in Hebrew poetry as something entirely distinguishable from parallelism itself.[34] Others we have mentioned limit grammatic parallelism almost exclusively to syntactic levels.[35] Still others, such as Berlin, who have been influenced strongly by linguistic theorists such as Roman Jakobson, will distinguish grammatic, lexical, and semantic as well as phonologic.

Because of the way they are translated in English, morphologic parallelisms are difficult for the non-Hebrew reader to identify. The simplest example of the problem can be observed by noting that in English, gender is not indicated by different morphologic endings. On the other hand, Hebrew nouns indicate gender by different endings for masculine plurals as well as for feminine singulars and plurals. Despite the fact that some of these morphologic parallelisms are difficult for the non-Hebrew reader to recognize, one needs to be aware of the tremendous range of options that Hebrew poetry had at its disposal to further parallelism. Morphologic contrasts and equivalences do not call attention to word order but to the substitution of words in one colon for functionally equivalent words in another colon. These contrasts or equivalences can be articulated through gender (masculine or feminine), number (singular and/or plural), definiteness ("the" or "a"), conjugation, tense, and a number of other elements. The following examples are illustrative of several kinds of morphologic parallelism that are observable to the English reader.

1. Number

The singular, "innocent individual," in the A colon is contrasted with the plural, "upright ones," in the B colon:

A   Think now, what innocent individual perishes;
B   or where the upright ones have been ruined?
Job 4:7*

The singular, "father," is contrasted with the plural, "elders":

A   Ask your father, and he will inform you;
B   your elders, and they will tell you.
Deut. 32:7

2. Tense

The perfect in the A colon is contrasted with the imperfect in the B colon:

A   The LORD at the flood sat enthroned;
B   The LORD sits enthroned, king forever.
Ps. 29:10*

3. Proper noun and pronoun

In the A colon, "LORD," a proper noun, is used, and a pronoun substitutes for "LORD" in the B colon.

A   Praise the LORD with the lyre;
B   make melody to him with the harp of ten strings.
Ps. 33:2

These morphologically diverse parallelisms draw our attention to the semantic correspondences. The semantic parallelism in each of the examples is enforced by grammatic parallelism.

Among some of the other types of morphologic parallelism more problematic for the English reader are the following: a masculine noun in one colon and a feminine noun in the other colon (Prov. 14:13; Jer 46:12), sometimes referred to as gender parallelism; a kind of voice or conjugational parallelism that uses an active construction in one colon and in the next a passive conjugation (Ps. 24:7).

While morphologic parallelism focuses more on the word or lexical element, other types of grammatic parallelism hinge on syntactic levels. One of these has been identified as gapping, ellipsis, or deletion. By paying careful attention to the individual words that make up each of the cola, one can notice that a word is missing, usually from the second colon. Nonetheless the force of that word in the first colon carries into the second colon. Again we examine the Deut. 32:7 example, which also exhibited morphologic parallelism:

> Ask your father, and he will inform you;
> your elders, and they will tell you.

The imperative "ask" is not stated in the second colon; nonetheless its semantic force is presumed. Jeremiah 51:31 (Watson's translation) serves as another example of gapping. The verb ("does run") carries into the second colon. Just as runners run to meet runners, so do messengers run to meet messengers:

> Runner to meet runner, does run,
> messenger to meet messenger.

Psalm 78:51 carries the force of the verb "struck" from the first colon to the second:

> He struck all the firstborn in Egypt,
> the first issue of their strength in the tents of Ham.

"All the firstborn" and "the first issue of their strength" are equivalent.

These examples show how attention to syntactic matters assist the interpreter in identifying parallelism at work with and beyond the semantic level. At a semantic level in gapping one can also detect a number of paradigmatic elements. For example, the "firstborn" and the "first issue" certainly have a kind of paradigmatic relationship.

In addition to the above types of grammatic parallelism, we suggest that the interpreter capable of reading Hebrew be aware of phonetic or phonologic parallelism and repetition. These features will enforce other aspects of parallelism. Berlin has developed the argument for phonologic parallelism. She defines it as "the repetition in parallel words or lines of the same or similar consonants in any order within close proximity."[36] Sometimes one dimension of phonological parallelism is referred to as alliteration, that is, the repetition of a consonant. It has been observed that the letter "q" occurs eight times in the short span of Joel 2:15-16.[37] A variety of issues (historical and linguistic) associated with the Hebrew vowel system make assonance, that is, the repetition of a vowel, an even more debated issue. In any case, these phonologic dimensions of parallelism are especially difficult for the non-Hebrew reader.

SUMMARY

In summary, several factors are essential for us to identify Hebrew parallelism and to use an understanding of it in the interpretation of poetry. First, Lowth was correct: parallelism is a matter of correspondence. There is, however, considerable variety in identifying what is at the heart of the correspondence. Some scholars demand that the correspondence be construed rather strictly, taking grammatical identity between A and B as the single criterion. This, of course, would rule out much of what Lowth deemed to be synthetic parallelism. One of the valuable recent contributors, E. Greenstein, contends that parallelism exists only where one has strict identity or repetition in the syntactic patterning of a sentence.[38] He relies entirely on grammatical identity at the level of deep structure.

Others delineate new categories to unravel what is at the heart of the correspondence. For example, Watson states that parallelism "belongs within a larger group of mathematical analogues and cannot be exalted to the rank of 'the characteristic of Hebrew poetry.'"[39] His chapter on parallelism is divided into six categories: gender-matched, word-pairs, number, staircase, noun-verb, and "Janus" parallelism.[40] Geller uses another set of six categories to delineate parallelism: synonym, list, antonym, merism, identity, and metaphor. These various attempts at categorization use semantic and grammatic elements, but they seem to run the risk of being mere revisions of Lowth's categories. They neither better state what is at the heart of the correspondence nor assist the interpreter in using the identification of parallelism to understand a poem better.

34

We take a very broad understanding of parallelism. It occurs in the interaction of semantic and grammatic equivalence and opposition. The juxtaposition of an A and B provides the opportunity for an almost infinite number of correspondences. The equivalence or opposition within the correspondence may be furthered at grammatic and semantic levels. "A is so, and *what's more*, B is so"[41] is too limiting a description of the correspondence. A is related to B at a multiplicity of grammatic and semantic levels. The correspondence of A and B is not merely A + B, nor A > B, nor A < B. As one recent contributor to the discussion has said, "The whole [bicolon] is different from the sum of its parts because the parts influence and contaminate each other."[42] Parallelism is not something that is predictable, and no mechanical system or set of categories can confine it. Rather, we must carefully observe the individual words as well as their relationships at the level of the colon, multi-colon, and entire poem in order to comprehend the range of parallelisms utilized in the Hebrew Bible.

3
Meter and Rhythm

It is common to associate poetry with the presence of meter. However, even the reader of English-language poetry knows that some poets practice their art without using meter—for example, the free verse of Ezra Pound. In addition, there is considerable debate about meter in Hebrew poetry. A number of recent analyses of Hebrew poetry argue that meter per se is not present.[1] Others dispute this judgment. Consequently, it is necessary that one think critically about the notions of meter and rhythm before commenting on the presence of either in classical Hebrew poetry.

In the previous chapter we argued that the notion of parallelism may be understood more accurately and fully by employing the analytical categories that derive from the study of grammar. As we proceed to a discussion of meter and rhythm, it will be useful to continue this same perspective. Put another way, it is appropriate that one use the discrete categories that derive from grammatical analysis when investigating the complex issues of rhythm and meter. One should note that the categories of morphology and phonology, and particularly those of accent or stress, are important for an assessment of rhythm in Hebrew poetry.

DEFINITIONS

In order to provide some measure of uniformity at the beginning of this discussion, we understand rhythm to be "a cadence, a contour, a figure of periodicity, any sequence perceptible as a distinct pattern capable of repetition and variation."[2] On the other hand, meter may be construed as "more or less regular poetic rhythm; the measurable rhythmical patterns manifested in verse, or the 'ideal' patterns which poetic rhythms approximate. . . . If meter is regarded as the ideal rhythmical pattern, then 'rhythm' becomes meter the closer it approaches regularity and predictability."[3] Meter may be viewed as a subspecies of rhythm, one that occurs within the poetic provenance.[4]

Another term prominent in many discussions of Hebrew poetry is "prosody." Prosody has often been used as if it were synonymous with metrics, that is, some scholars write as if they thought prosodic analysis equals metrical analysis. But prosody involves more than a description of meter. Again, we use the *Princeton Handbook* as a touchstone: "Prosody is the most general term used to refer to the elements and structure involved in the rhythmic or dynamic aspect of speech. . . . Literary prosody studies the rhythmic structure of prose and verse."[5] Hence it is misleading to speak of prosody or prosodic analysis and mean by that metrics or study of rhythm only in poetic texts.

Prosodic analysis typically eventuates in the identification of rhythmic structures, whether something relatively loose, like cadence, or something very regular, like meter. In such rhythmic structures the primary variables are those of intensity, duration, and pitch. If one highlights the factor of duration, then, when analyzing Hebrew poetry, one would end up counting syllables. If, on the other hand, one were focusing on intensity, then one would count stresses or accents. As a result, it is important to be clear about the distinction between meter and prosody, since scholars using these two categories may end up pursuing quite different forms of analysis.

Most theories about Hebrew prosody and meter identify one or another recurring element in the poetic line, for example, repetition in the numbers of syllables or in the numbers of stresses or accents. Much of the debate about the presence of meter or the various types of metrical systems hinges on precisely what it is in the language that is being repeated. It is possible to maintain that there are four primary types of meter: "the syllabic, the accentual, the accentual-syllabic, and the quantitative."[6] From this perspective, debates about meter in Hebrew poetry may be viewed as debates over whether Hebrew poetry involves syllabic or accentual meter, that is, over whether what is being repeated is essentially numbers of syllables or numbers of stressed words.

METER

Having broached some of the basic terms that appear in discussions of meter—meter, rhythm, prosody, accent, and stress—we are now in a position to address the question of meter in Hebrew. That Hebrew poetry includes meter is a notion that dates to the Greco-Roman period. As Gray and Kugel among others have observed, Philo and Josephus maintained that meter was present in Hebrew poetry. In Philo's case, the claim probably refers to postbiblical Hebrew texts. With Josephus, however, the assertion deals specifically with biblical poetry, namely, that it was composed according to certain metrical constraints, which he understood according to the principles of meter in Greek poetry. He once wrote, "And now David . . . composed songs and hymns to God of several sorts of meter; some of these he made with trimeter, some pentameters."[7] The reasons for Josephus's judgment are surely complex, although one motive is obvious. For Jews interested in defending the excellence of their religious poetry in a culture that defined poetry, at least in part, in terms of meter, it was appropriate to maintain that their canon's poetry was metric in character as well.

This contention, that Hebrew poetry was metric, continued with surprising vigor over the centuries. Scholars such as Origen and Jerome argued that one may identify meter in various poetic sections of the Hebrew Bible. In our judgment, however, no attempt, whether by ancient or modern scholars, to identify the presence of something like classic Greek metric forms in Hebrew poetry has proved successful.[8]

Because it has been difficult, if not impossible, to discern a metrical system in Hebrew poetry, some scholars have revised the notion of meter itself to accommodate the data presented in the Masoretic text. As a result, no recent treatment that makes a claim for the presence of meter in Hebrew poetry has argued the case for metric patterns of the sort found in Greek, Latin, or English poetry. Put another way, although contemporary Hebrew Bible scholars may include discussion of meter within their treatments of Hebrew poetry, they typically do not understand this meter as fundamentally similar to that of Greek, Latin, or English poetry.

If by meter one means various forms of rhythmic regularity, however, then the search could go on for regularity of a sort different from, for example, iambic pentameter. In the case of biblical Hebrew, scholars have claimed to find regularity based on the patterns of Hebrew accentuation.[9] This regularity is said to be based not on the presence of a series of unaccented and then accented syllables, as is the case with classic Greek meter, but rather on the repetition of the number of accents in parallel lines.[10] This scansion is based on the fact that in Hebrew each word has its own accent. So, for example, in Isa. 5:3b, the line "judge between me" contains two accents, and so too does the ensuing line, "and my vineyard." Some scholars have described that bicolon as one constructed according to a 2 + 2 meter. Such an assessment is based on a count of the word accents in the Hebrew text. An alternate system, one often associated with the names of Cross and, especially, Freedman, focuses on the number of syllables in a particular colon or bicolon. In the case of Isa. 5:3, the syllable count is 5 + 4. This particular form of analysis may be quite complicated, since it is sometimes deemed necessary to reconstruct the syllabification of the Hebrew word in order to make it reflect the presumed form of the word that would have existed when the poem was composed.

A metrical scansion (to scan is to analyze poetry by counting accents or syllables) based on an assessment of word accentuation has enabled scholars to provide numeric, "metrical" analyses of Hebrew texts. So, for example, Hans Wildberger analyzes the structure of Isa. 5:1-7 in the following way:[11]

v. 1	3 + 3, 3 + 2
v. 2	2 + 2, 3 + 2, 3 + 2
v. 3	3 + 2, 3 + 2
v. 4	2 + 2 + 2, 2 + 2 + 2
v. 5a	4 + 4
v. 5b	2 + 2, 2 + 2
v. 6	(2) 3 + 3, 3 + 3
v. 7	3 + 2, 2 + 2, 2 + 2, 1 + 2

At the minimum, one may say two things about this form of analysis. First, capable scholars disagree over the particulars of accent-based scansion.[12] It is possible to analyze Isa. 5:2 as comprising 3 + 3, 3 + 3, 3 + 3 or 2 + 2, 3 + 2, 3 + 2. Much depends on what one thinks might be the possible minimum length of the poetic line or colon. Another variable is, of course, whether one scans syllables or accents. The key issue in Isa. 5:2 involves the first colon. Does it have the same weight, whether determined by accent or syllable, as does the second? In transliteration the verse reads as follows:

> way'azzĕqēhû (he digged it) waysaqqĕlēhû (he cleared it of stones)
> wayyiṭṭā'ēhû (he planted it) śōrēq (with choice vines)

If one follows the view that each word has only one accent, then a 2 + 2, 2 + 2 pattern is clearly evident. If one focuses on syllables, then the first colon is decidedly longer: ten syllables in the first, seven syllables in the second. (And since a 3 + 2 pattern is evident in the rest of vv. 1-2, one is tempted strongly to construe the colon in question so that it will agree with the pattern present in surrounding bicola.) But there is a second and more fundamental issue. Even if individuals agree on one accentual scansion, one must ask if such an accentual pattern truly identifies meter. Or, put in a slightly different way, does Wildberger's scansion reveal a rhythmic structure consistent throughout the text and, in fact, consistent with other stylistic features of the text?[13] In our judgment, the answer to both questions is no. There are no regular and predictable patterns of rhythm.

Some scholars have redefined meter so that it may be used to describe classical Hebrew poetry. Such efforts, however, make the notion of meter mean something quite different from what that term normally describes. Hence these revisions deprive the term of its normal explanatory power. The terms "mixed meter" and "irregular meter" do not clarify the matter.[14]

"Mixed meter" is used to describe the occurrence of bicola and tricola in a poem, each of which may have an accentual pattern different from what precedes or follows it. For example, a two-accent bicolon may follow a three-accent bicolon. "Irregular meter" is used to describe differences within the bicolon or tricolon itself. One might think of a tricolon made up of two three-accented lines followed by a two-accent line. In neither case, "mixed meter" or "irregular meter," does the poem present rhythmic constructions of the sort that would typically be described as meter.

Consequently, it would be wise to avoid the language of meter in favor of the broader term "rhythm" for Hebrew poetry. Seymour Chatman, in a seminal work on meter and rhythm, quotes the following typical and recent definition of rhythm. It is "the serial recurrence of a given time interval or group of time intervals marked off by sounds."[15] By way of contrast, "meter is basically linguistically determined 'secondary rhythm'—linguistic events grouped regularly in time, such that each group has unity in its internal composition and in its external relations."[16] On the basis of these definitions, one may note that a key issue in the decision about the presence of meter in any text involves a judgment about the regularity of the linguistic, especially phonetic, events that occur in the poetic line as well as the extent to which such regularity provides for unity throughout the composition. If, for example, one finds a poem with an accentual pattern of 2 + 2,

3 + 3, 2 + 2, does such a rhythmic pattern count as meter? In our judgment, one should answer this question in the negative. Despite the regularity with which lines that may be construed as 2 + 2 or 3 + 3 occur, the ordering of such lines within one poem or among multiple poems is so haphazard as to disallow the notion of meter.

An increasing number of scholars share the judgment that meter cannot be observed in Hebrew poetry. Both Kugel and O'Connor argue against the presence of meter in Hebrew, although from quite different perspectives. Kugel writes: "Nearly two thousand years of scanning, syllable-counting, and the like have failed to yield a consistent metric structure."[17] O'Connor is equally decisive: "We have proposed that no consensus had ever been reached in the matter of Hebrew meter because there is none."[18] Collins too, although attempting to identify some basic syntactic, one might even say rhythmic, patterns in Hebrew, hesitates to describe them as meter.[19] Alter also expresses reservations about discerning meter in Hebrew as if it were in any essential way similar to meter known in ancient Greek or Latin poetry: "And so the term meter should probably be abandoned for biblical verse."[20] Pardee, as well, demurs about finding meter in either Ugaritic or Hebrew poetry: "Neither of the two primary meanings of the term 'meter' is properly ascribed to Ugaritic and Hebrew poetry: that these poetic systems do not have anything corresponding to the classical foot, and that there is not discernible in them a 'predominant form of rhythm.'"[21] Even earlier expositions provide only guarded affirmations about the presence of meter in classical Hebrew: "The metric hypotheses rest upon a combination of inference from parallelism and application of the Masoretic accents, rather than on any intrinsic evidence from biblical Hebrew."[22] On the basis of these judgments, made as they are from a significant variety of theoretical perspectives, it is possible to discern an emerging scholarly consensus that denies the existence of meter in classical Hebrew poetry.

In sum, it seems appropriate to delete meter as a category for understanding biblical Hebrew poetry. Rather, the language of rhythm and rhythmic patterns is more consistent with the texts in view. So, for example, Alter speaks about the "free rhythm" of biblical versification.[23] However, to use the language of rhythm instead of meter is not new; thus Johann Döller, "Biblical Hebrew poetry is rhythmic, but not metric."[24]

Most linguists would maintain that human language, including poetry, inherently involves rhythm, even patterns of rhythm. The presence of such patterns—for example, in the way that one typically pronounces the phrase "Auf Wiedersehen"—does not, however, mean that all human utterance is metric, even poetic. Nonetheless it is correct to conclude that poetry, as human utterance, is rhythmic. The task of defining rhythmic variety and regularity as they are manifest in Hebrew poetry and without forcing such variety and regularity into the analytical categories of meter constitutes the task at hand.

RHYTHM

The perspective expressed here stems from the so-called Ley-Budde-Sievers tradition, with closest ties to the work of Julius Ley, namely, the primary data used in an assessment of Hebrew rhythm is provided by accented syllables. Even though we affirm the Ley-Budde-Sievers tradition, analysis of Hebrew poetry based on stress or accent presents problems. There are at least two reasons for the use of caution when one examines accented syllables. First, the Masoretic text includes a complicated system of primary and secondary accentuation markings, a system that is considerably later than the poems themselves. Second, during the earliest period that the Hebrew poetry was being created, there were several major developments in the language that affected the position of accents on given words. For example, in the languages spoken in Syria-Palestine during the Late Bronze Age, case endings were present on nouns. The word for "word" in the nominative case would have been written *dabaru*, with the *u* serving as the nominative case ending. During the transition from the Late Bronze Age to the Early Iron Age, these case endings fell out of use. Through a process of conditioned phonetic change, the syllabic structure and stress of words that had occurred with case endings became different. So the word for "word" became *dābār*, with the accent on the second syllable of the word instead of the first syllable as it had earlier. Any poem that had the word "word" in it would now sound different. Such is one example of the history of change in the Hebrew language. Despite this development, the very fact that the word for "word," whether *dabaru* or *dābār*, had one accent allows us to capture something of essential importance in the language, something that enables us to identify, even today, patterns of rhythm that are constituent for ancient Hebrew poetry.

We propose to use the term "rhythmic patterns" as a way of thinking about and describing rhythm in Hebrew poetry.[25] Such patterns may

43

be discerned on the basis of careful attention to the occurrence of stressed or accented words in Hebrew poetry. Rhythmic patterns in poetry typically involve four elements: regularity, variation, grouping, and hierarchy.[26] These four elements have been identified in the poetry of many languages. Precisely how do these elements work in Hebrew poetry?

As for the first category, regularity, Hebrew poets composed lines of similar length. This similarity of line length created parallel lines, the regularity of which is based on regular occurrences of stress, for example, 2 + 2, 3 + 3. These groupings of at least two poetic lines may be described as rhythmic patterns. A two-accent bicolon is one sort of rhythmic pattern, and a three-accent tricolon is a different kind of rhythmic pattern. Such balance between parallel lines provided the rhythmic regularity that one normally associates with poetry.

The second category, variation, occurs primarily as a result of the number of syllables present in the coordinate cola. Put another way, in a bicolon that appears regular because of the primary accentual pattern, there is some variety because the number of syllables in the two lines normally varies. For example, in Isa. 5:1 the first bicolon comprises a 3 + 3 accentually defined rhythmic pattern. As such, it may be viewed as "regular." If one counts syllables, however, one discerns a bicolon with seven syllables in the first line and six in the second line. Variety occurs within a regular structure.

Third, the notion of grouping is directly related to the first category, that of regularity. The very existence of a rhythmic pattern presupposes a beginning and an end of the pattern. In Hebrew poetry, there are really two basic forms of grouping: the grouping of words that forms the individual poetic line, typically two or three accented words, and the grouping of bicola and tricola. In this regard, "the most natural groupings [in Hebrew poetry, we should think of accent-based patterns] seem to be twos and threes, the prime numbers which can be added together or repeated in various combinations to produce every possible larger group."[27] As a result, it is surely no accident that the primary rhythmic patterns in biblical Hebrew are 2 + 2 and 3 + 3, given the prominence of these numbers in the poetry of various languages.

The integrity of the grouping is created by the phenomenon of "end-stopping."[28] There is typically some form of grammatical stop at the end of each poetic line. Such stops are often, although not always, indicated by a comma or a semicolon in English translation. For example, Isa. 24:19 presents a tricolon in which each Hebrew line has three accents:

> The earth is utterly broken,
> the earth is torn asunder,
> the earth is violently shaken.

The punctuation present in this translation is, of course, not present in the Hebrew text. Such punctuation is required in a translation, however, to express the rhythmic groupings present in the poem. There is a full end stop at the end of the verse, as indicated by the period. After each line, there is a comma, which indicates a less powerful stop, one that identifies the end of the line but not the end of the rhythmic pattern. Scholars describe such stops in various ways. O'Connor's language is rather technical, "medial caesura," which he uses to describe the end stop that occurs at the end of a line. Kugel's terminology is less technical, namely, "slight pause" and "full pause."

The phenomenon of end-stopping in Hebrew grows out of the syntactic units, which conclude in identifiable ways. Parallelism is crucial in determining the end stops.[29] Semantic parallelism, as in the example of Isa. 24:19, often assists in the creation of end-stopping. In the Hebrew text of this verse, the word "earth" occurs at the end of each of the three lines. In addition, Hebrew phonology allows for the creation of so-called "pausal" forms, words that have a slightly different structure when they occur at the end of a sentence or poetic line. So, for example, in Jer. 22:29 there is a brief poetic line:

> O land, land, land,
> hear the word of the LORD!

The word "land" in Hebrew is normally written ʿereṣ, and so it is in the first two occurrences in this first line of the bicolon. At the end of this line, however, the word is written ʾāreṣ. The "a" vowel signifies a pausal form, which one would expect to occur at the end of the poetic line. In sum, semantics, syntax, or phonology may contribute to the creation of end-stopping.

The fourth and last category important for analysis of rhythmic structures is hierarchy. Hierarchy may be defined as "patterns on lower levels of rhythmic series that are frequently repeated across wider spans on higher levels."[30] Of the four elements used in discussing rhythmic structures, this is the least important in Hebrew poetry, but it can be recognized. The phenomenon of what some have called external parallelism, namely, correspondences between various bicola, presents a graphic example of hierarchy in classical Hebrew, for example, Isa. 1:3:

> The ox knows its owner,
> and the donkey its master's crib;
> but Israel does not know,
> my people do not understand.

These two bicola stand in what Norman Gottwald termed "external antithetic parallelism." This label means that there are two bicola, each of which involves internal synonymous (in at least semantic terms) parallelism. However, when these two bicola are juxtaposed, they create a new and larger structure, which involves antithetic (again in semantic terms) parallelism.

Hierarchy does not appear to be as significant an element in the creation and function of the rhythmic pattern in Hebrew poetry as do regularity, variation, and grouping. It may well be that the relative unimportance of hierarchy inhibits the strong sense of formal or structural coherence in some Hebrew poems, something that we have repeatedly found to be the case.

Rhythmic patterns of various sorts occur within single poems, for example, 2 + 2, 3 + 3, or 3 + 2 sequences. However, identical sequences recur infrequently, that is, a sequence of 2 + 2, 2 + 2, 2 + 2, 2 + 2. If one looks, for example, at Wildberger's scansion of Isa. 5:1-7, one discovers that the longest sequence of a repeated accentual pattern occurs four times, 3 + 2 in vv. 2-3.[31] Some Hebrew poetry does offer far more significant evidence for the repetition of identical rhythmic patterns, for example, Psalm 29 with its predominately 2 + 2 pattern. Most classical Hebrew poetry, however, such as that found in the Book of Job, is made up of combinations of diverse rhythmic patterns. Repetition of identical patterns, unlike repetition of lines in iambic pentameter, does not typically provide coherence or unity for an entire Hebrew poem. Rather, diversity among patterns provides variety within the poem, especially in poems that involve various types of similarity or synonymity.

Hebrew poetry is marked by a delicate balance between regularity and variation. The rhythmic pattern itself allows for both qualities: regularity of stress as in a 2 + 2 bicolon; and variation, either diverse rhythmic patterns in one poem or semantic opposition or contrast within one bicolon. The rhythmic patterns available to the Hebrew poet function something like building blocks. There are a finite number of frequent rhythmic patterns, basically two- and three-accent bicola and tricola. Out of these limited but nonetheless rich structural possibilities, individual writers were able to compose poems of astonishing formal and rhythmic variety, even in as short a piece as Isa. 5:1-7.

Rhythm in Hebrew poetry works in a way quite distinct from the way in which meter is often understood to function in the poetry of many other languages. Literary critics often note that meter in a Greek or English poem provides unity or overall coherence in the work. For example, repeated lines in heroic verse provide stylistic glue. The case with rhythmic patterns in classical Hebrew poetry is more complex, involving both regularity and variety. Use of diverse rhythmic patterns in one poem provides for variety, not consistency, within one Hebrew poem. As a result, to attribute the role of meter to what we have described as rhythmic patterns would be fundamentally to misconstrue one important aspect of Hebrew verse. Hence, simply to dissolve the link between meter and Hebrew poetry allows for a fresh understanding of that literature. Rather than seeking or expecting the sort of uniformity that meter typically generates in poems written in other languages, one anticipates a delicate balance between regularity and variation.

In sum, Hebrew poetry possesses rhythm, not meter. Such rhythm, often described in rhythmic patterns, is distinctive because it functions differently from meter. As a result, one may read Hebrew poetry looking for both rhythmic regularity and variety, not metric predictability.

4
Poetic Style

To devote so much attention to the issues of parallelism and rhythm in a basic discussion of Hebrew poetry may seem odd to the student of English poetry. Considerations of theme, imagery, figurative language, perhaps even poetic diction, would have been expected much earlier in the analysis. These topics have, in fact, become increasingly prominent in the study of Hebrew poetry.[1]

We will consider two literary devices other than parallelism and rhythm—namely, simile and stanza—under the rubric of style. This is by no means a comprehensive listing of all stylistic devices. Moreover, the category of style is not without its problems.[2] For some analysts, style is something that inheres within the entire poem; for others, one or another element in the poem constitutes a stylistic feature, for example, a particular metaphor. For some, style is characteristic of a particular author, for example, Pope's style; for others, style describes commonalities between several authors' works in a given period, for example, Elizabethan tragedies. Although all these uses are appropriate, style in this context refers to the elements that the poet employs, including parallelism and rhythm, to create a particular poem. In a very real sense, the previous two chapters have been dealing in unusual focus with matters of Hebrew poetic style. Such treatment was necessary because those two topics, parallelism and rhythm, have been so prominent in the history of reflection upon Hebrew poetry. However, various forms of parallelism and rhythmic patterns are only two among many stylistic features of Hebrew poetry.

Of the stylistic elements we discuss in this chapter, the first could and does appear in prose as well as in poetry. To that extent such elements are not, in an exclusive way, poetic. As we pointed out in chapter 1, however, poetry is literature in which such elements appear in a particularly rich and concentrated, one might even say constitutive, way. Just as parallelism and rhythm occur both in poetry and in prose, so too do some of the elements considered here.

SIMILE

The first stylistic element, the simile, is common to poetry the world over. A simile is a figure of speech in which two entities are compared. The comparison is normally created morphologically, namely, by an indicator of resemblance, such as the word "like" or "as." A typical simile might be: This rainbow trout glistens like fire. A simile differs from a metaphor, another figure of speech in which two entities are compared, by having an identifiable indicator of resemblance. A metaphor has no such explicit indicator, for example: The fish is a stroke of lightning. In the cases of both metaphor and simile, one may, using the vocabulary of I. A. Richards, speak of tenor and vehicle. "The tenor is the idea being expressed or the subject of the comparison; the vehicle is the image by which this idea is conveyed or the subject communicated."[3] In the example of the simile used earlier in this paragraph, the coloration of the fish is the tenor and fire is the vehicle, whereas in the metaphor, the speed of the fish is the tenor and lightning is the vehicle.

The distinction between simile and metaphor, however, involves more than the mechanical presence of an explicit indicator. Harold Fisch maintains that "simile distances tenor and vehicle, metaphor approximates them."[4] Nonetheless, at least on semantic grounds, Berlin has argued, "It is but a small step from simile to metaphor."[5] For our purpose, however, the presence of a grammatical marker, not semantic considerations, will serve primarily to identify a simile.

Because similes are so prominent in Hosea, it is appropriate to treat similes in this prophetic book as an exemplary poetic trope. In biblical Hebrew, several particles or words may be used as the indicator of resemblance, that is, kě ("like"), māšal ("become like"), 'îm ("like").[6] However, in Hosea's poetry, only kě or kěmô is used. In Hos. 4–14, such particles occur over forty times to introduce a simile (we exclude 13:15, "as the reed plant," since this translation requires a conjectural emendation of the Hebrew text).[7]

Several observations may help the reader understand and appreciate Hosea's similes.[8] First, the vast majority of vehicles that Hosea employs come from the world of nature. Rain (6:3), birds (11:11), animals (13:7), and plants (10:4) populate the clauses introduced by the indicators of resemblance.[9] Such imagery is not surprising, since Hosea was involved in a radical critique of Baalistic religion, which involved the claim that Baal was responsible for fecundity in the natural order. There is less variety in the tenors. Either Yahweh's positive (6:3) or punitive action (5:12) or Israel's malfeasance (7:6-7) provides the standard subjects.[10]

Second, and more fundamental, there is remarkable diversity in the ways in which Hosea's similes function. One may begin to recognize this diversity by noting that there is structural variety in the similes. Some may work within a single line or colon:

> his appearing is as sure as the dawn
> Hos. 6:3

Others occur within a single bicolon, wherein the first line provides the tenor and the second line the vehicle:

> Samaria's king shall perish
> like a chip on the face of the waters.
> Hos. 10:7

More frequently, however, several similes are constructed in parallel lines, for example, Hos. 5:14a. The repetition of the indicator of resemblance ("like"), the repeated preposition ("to"), and the identical word order create morphologic and phonologic parallelism. Syntactically, gapping often exists; the second colon depends on the first colon's use of the personal pronoun "I."

> For I will be like a lion to Ephraim
> and like a young lion to the house of Judah.
> Hos. 5:14[11]

Despite the structural diversity of the above-mentioned similes, each presents a paradigmatic equivalence, that is, a substitution through the use of the vehicle. The vehicle or parallel vehicles capture one or more salient features of the tenor: the regularity and brilliance of the dawn expresses Yahweh's military appearance; the demise of a king before Yahweh is as inconsequential and easily achieved as is the

51

bouncing of a wood chip on, and then its disappearance in, the sea; the powerful and devouring lions exemplify Yahweh's response to Ephraim.

However, not all of Hosea's similes are so straightforward in structure or meaning. On the one hand, there are relatively short and yet complex similes:

> Like a stubborn heifer
>   stubborn is Israel,
> will Yahweh feed them;
>   like a lamb in a broad pasture?
>   Hos. 4:16*

This pair of bicola comprises two similes, the second builds on the first. This is similar to the syntagmatic relationships considered in chapter 2 on parallelism. The comparison of Israel to an animal is made, then the one feeding the animal (Yahweh) is named, and finally the location of feeding is identified. Moreover, the bicola are chiastically structured: vehicle-tenor, tenor-vehicle. The subject in the first simile is the proper noun, "Israel," which finds its equivalent expressed in the second simile as an object pronoun, "them." The noun-pronoun and subject-object provide a morphologic parallelism. The substitution of the pronoun for the noun suggests a paradigmatic relationship (cf. chapter 2 on parallelism). The reader anticipates a synonymous tenor. However, different vehicles, "heifer" and "lamb," are used within these tight confines. The first ("heifer") is feminine, although it more frequently appears as a masculine noun (Hos. 14:3). The second vehicle ("lamb") is masculine, although it also can appear in the feminine gender (2 Sam. 12:3, 4, 6). This gender contrast enforces the other grammatic parallelisms, suggesting that there is not mere substitution but progression of thought. Israel's stubbornness is highlighted specifically in the first simile by the repetition of the word *srr*, "stubborn." This word is most often used to describe willful children, thus developing, along with the connotations of "heifer," the idea of youthful rebels. However, the second bicolon, with its new vehicle, treats Yahweh's willingness to act as shepherd toward a lamb. Furthermore, the second simile is carved out as a rhetorical question, with a presumed negative answer. This presumption depends on the first simile, namely, Yahweh will not feed them because of their stubbornness. Put another way, the negative answer to the second simile depends on the point of the first simile. Without the first bicolon, one might be tempted to answer affirmatively the question embedded in the second bicolon. This second bicolon exhibits external and contrasting, morphologic parallelism. The indicative mood of the first bicolon is developed syntagmatically through the interrogative mood of the second bicolon.

Finally, the two similes are related as indictment to sentence. Because Israel has been stubborn, they will not be fed and, presumably, will become malnourished and die. Within this development, there is an element of semantic continuity, namely, the heifer-lamb conveys the dominant image of youthfulness, which may involve stubbornness and palpable hunger.

Hosea also creates some long and complex similes. The editors of Hosea have placed multiple similes near the end of the book. The first involves two oracles of judgment, Hos. 13:1-3 and 13:4-8. In both cases, the indictments, vv. 1-2 and 4-6, include virtually no figurative language. However, in both cases, the sentences, vv. 3 and 7-8, comprise lengthy similes. For the interpretation of these individual oracles, it is important to assess the way these similes work individually and then together.

The first oracle indicts Ephraim for Baal veneration and for the use of images in religious ritual. This indictment is expressed in direct language, for example, the making of molten images. The character of the poetry changes radically in v. 3.

> Therefore they shall be like the morning mist
> or like the dew that goes away early,
> like chaff that swirls from the threshing floor
> or like smoke (rising) from a window.

Following the particle *lākēn*, "therefore," which often introduces the sentence portion of a judgment oracle, there are four clauses in which an indicator of resemblance introduces a separate simile. In these similes the repeated indicator as well as the preposition "from," which is drawn in the second bicolon, provides morphologic and phonologic parallelism. By contrast, there is a chiastic form of grammatic parallelism, which links the elements syntactically. The first and last similes are made up of nominal clauses, whereas the middle two similes are verbal clauses. One might argue that the verb of the second simile controls the first, that is, the mist goes away early, and that the verb of the third simile controls the fourth, that is, that the smoke swirls.

The sentence that governs these similes is straightforward: "They will be like . . . " However, the subject of the similes is not altogether clear. The indictment is, of course, directed against the people for perpetrating practices inimical to Yahweh. Hence the "they" could be the people. Such an interpretation would appear to fit the logic of a judgment oracle. It would be more proper grammatically, and perhaps semantically as well, to identify the "they" with the idols in which the people have put their trust. In either case, some party or object is depicted in similes that emphasize transience or impermanence. The first pair of similes had occurred earlier in the book, in Hos. 6:4 ("like a morning cloud, like the dew"). There, however, they functioned as an indictment. The tenor was Israel's love, which the similes depicted as impermanent. These vehicles function differently in 13:3, where they are part of the sentence. Either Israel or the idols will vanish like the morning cloud, like the dew that disappears early in the morning. Both vehicles point to evanescent water, mist or dew, that vanishes during the course of the day. Rather than suggesting simple impermanence, however, the simile works to report punitive removal. The simile in 13:3, therefore, works in a quite different way from 6:4 because the tenors are different; in Hosea 6, the author focuses on the people's love, in Hosea 13 on religious malfeasance, and this despite the identical wording of the similes. The emphasis in 6:4 is on the impermanence of the people's affection for Yahweh, whereas the emphasis in 13:3 is on the ease with which the removal, whether of people or of idols, can be accomplished.

Hosea 13:3 includes two more similes, "like chaff that swirls from the threshing floor/ like smoke (rising) from a window//." There is no verb in the second colon (e.g., gapping), thus creating some ambiguity. If the first two similes present something of a pair, so also do the last two. Instead of something that disappears, the focus shifts to things that are easily driven away by the wind. The tenor remains the same, but the vehicle has changed. They, the people or the idols, can be blown away as easily as chaff, as easily as smoke is blown away from a window, through which it leaves a building. The simile emphasizes active force against an object—wind on chaff, draft on smoke—rather than neutral disappearance as exemplified by the disappearance of dew. To that extent the second set of similes progresses, at least in its punitive connotation, beyond the first set. The people or the idols can be driven away easily, they do not simply disappear.

54

Hosea 13:3 provides two pairs of similes, each set providing a slightly different tenor. There are four vehicles—mist, dew, chaff, and smoke—and two tenors—people and idols. The two sets are ordered in a meaningful fashion, from neutral evaporation to something visible.

The second series of similes that is set within the sentence of a judgment oracle occurs in 13:7-8:

> So I will become like a lion to them,
>> like a leopard I will lurk beside the way.
> I will fall upon them like a bear robbed of her cubs,
>> and will tear open the covering of their heart;
> there I will devour them like a lion,
>> as a wild animal would mangle them.

Like the similes in 13:3, those in 13:7 commence with an image that had been used earlier in the book. In Hos. 5:14, the author creates two similes, both of which involve the lion as the vehicle: "I will be like a lion (*šaḥal*) to Ephraim, and like a young lion (*kĕpîr*) to the house of Judah." Then, using the figurative language of the simile, Yahweh reports his intent: "I, even I, will rend and go away, I will carry off, and none shall rescue." The similes in 13:7-8 commence with the statement, "so I will be to them like a lion," a clause that uses the same noun for lion, *šaḥal*, that was used in the first simile in 5:14. Unlike 5:14, however, the author of 13:7-8 explores Yahweh's punitive action by using a variety of animals rather than merely substituting Hebrew words for lion. Hosea uses four of the six Hebrew terms for lion (*'aryēh*, 11:10; *lābî'*, 13:8). The variety of ravaging beasts rather than one predator is a hallmark of these similes.

In Hos. 13:4-6, the indictment varied in its description of the guilty party. Sometimes it was "you" (vv. 4-5), but at the end of the indictment the poet had moved to less personal discourse, "they" (v. 6). And this third person rhetoric obtains in the judgment similes. The various animals are likened to "them." One senses that the simile and the third person rhetoric serve to distance Yahweh from those whom he will punish, since elsewhere, when Yahweh contemplates the destruction of Israel, and when he speaks about them in personal terms (so Hos. 11:9), God's heart recoils. By contrast, similes serve to distance the people from Yahweh and so enable Yahweh to contemplate their destruction.

One can recognize various kinds of grammatic and semantic development in the similes of Hos. 13:7-8. The first is created with the vehicle of the lion (*šaḥal*) and the tenor is again ambiguous. Yahweh will be a lion, but in what way? With the second simile, both tenor and vehicle are explicit. Yahweh will be like a leopard, the vehicle. And he will lurk, the tenor, along the roadside. Not only is a predator defined, but its ominous presence is localized. Still, however, the author does not mention the specific predacious act of the animal. That remains implicit in the second simile, just as did the tenor in the first simile.

In the third simile, matters develop further in two ways. First, the animal, in this case a bear, is especially vicious, since it is a bear that has lost its young. Second, for the first time the poet describes the predator's specific action, namely, ripping open the abdominal cavity of a person. This simile serves to elaborate the tenor, the particularly rapacious action of the predator animal. Even by the standards of animals thought to be dangerous, this attack would be especially vicious.

The fourth simile in the series provides something of a semantic if not phonetic inclusion. The animal is, as in the first simile, the lion, although with a different word for lion, *lābî'*. This linking of the fourth simile to the foregoing ones is enhanced by the presence of the word *šām*, "there," in the first colon. One is forced to contemplate the image of a lion coming upon the prey of a bear and then driving the bear away. Put another way, the presence of "there" creates a narrative quality in this sequence of similes. If the bear is the killer, then the lion is the devourer, the animal that completes the predatorial process until virtually nothing is left but carrion. Hence this tenor, the lion as devourer, is appropriate at this point in the series. In order to lend weight to this final act, the poet has depicted the lion as devourer with an implicit simile, that is, "as a wild beast would devour them," which, however, does not include the indicator of resemblance.[12]

In sum, this series of similes involving different animals provides a striking case of paradigmatic though subtle syntagmatic development, that is, there is not only substitution but also a building action. The grammatical repetition of the first person verbs and the indicators of resemblance suggests equivalence, especially with the lion inclusio. However, the character of the tenors builds the action, syntagmatically from the lurking presence, to the violent killing, and finally to eating. Through this series of similes, the poet conveys in clear and vivid language the violent fate that will befall the victim, Israel.

When one compares the similes of the two judgment oracles that occur in Hos. 13:1-8, one sees several sorts of pronounced development. There is a move within 13:3, from neutral dissolution to active removal. Then in 13:7-8 the predator similes denote Yahweh's active destruction. And within the similes of vv. 7-8 there is a progression, from animals, to animals lurking, to animals attacking, to animals devouring. Multiple similes allow for development or progression, a syntagmatic pattern common in this book.

The second major complex simile occurs in Hos. 14:4-8 (Heb., 14:5-9). It is surely the most complex simile construction in the entire book. In addition, its theme is unusual, since the topic is weal rather than woe for Israel. The rhetorical unit is larger than the simile. H. W. Wolff thinks the larger unit includes vv. 1-9, which is itself segmented into a prophetic summons (vv. 1-4) and a divine speech (vv. 5-9).[13] The simile occurs in, but does not exhaust, the divine speech. The speech, which commences in first person language, reports what Yahweh will do on Israel's behalf, namely, heal their erroneous ways and love them totally. However, after this initial tricolon, the deity begins to use the language of simile. The first simile, "I will be like the dew to Israel" (v. 5a), focuses on what the deity will do. The choice of words is remarkable. In Hos. 6:4, the same word, *tal*, "dew," was used in a simile to describe the unreliability of Israel's love. It is like dew because it disappears. In 14:4-5, the same vehicle occurs, as does the notion of love for the tenor. Here, however, the subject is Yahweh's, not Israel's, love. Because of this difference in tenor, *tal* or dew works differently as a vehicle from the way it worked in 6:4. On the basis of the ensuing similes, the reader learns that Yahweh as dew means fructifying water, which enables plants to blossom, germinate, and grow. A kind of syntagmatic progression develops within nearly identical grammatic structures of linked similes.

In the ensuing similes, Israel is personified and described by the use of botanical vocabulary. Beginning with the second colon of v. 5 and continuing through the end of v. 6, the poet speaks entirely within the realm of simile.

> He shall blossom like the lily,
>> He shall strike root as the poplar.
> His roots shall spread out;
> His beauty shall be like the olive,
>> and his fragrance like Lebanon.*

These lines are not grammatically synonymous, nor are they semantically identical. Just as there was progression of action in 13:7-8, so too there is development here. The poet describes Israel's reaction to Yahweh as dew by using the imagery of organic growth. And the poet diversifies this imagery. Instead of one plant, there are three: lily, poplar, and olive. Moreover, there is a meaningful order within the lexicography, from small plant to tree to larger tree. Also striking is the movement from the natural to the human perspectives. The language of the first three cola—blossoming, striking root, spreading root—is that of an emerging plant. However, the next two cola are evaluative, the sorts of evaluation that humans make—that something is beautiful to the eye and pleasant to the nostril. Put another way, the plant grows and matures, but it is also able to affect others when it is mature. Others may perceive the olive tree as delightful in various ways. The focus is decidedly unpragmatic. The olive tree is not valued because of the oil it produces but because of its beauty.

The poet moves out of the imagistic world in the first part of v. 7 and back to the vocabulary with which this rhetorical unit began, "return." However, the imperative rhetoric in v. 1, "Return!" now becomes predictive, "they shall return."[14] But as soon as the language of return has been adduced, the poet reintroduces symbolic language in which Yahweh casts a shadow.

> They shall return and dwell in his shadow,
>   they shall grow grain;
> they shall blossom like the vine,
>   his remembrance like the wine of Lebanon.*

There are numerous difficulties in the Hebrew text. Moreover, to what is Yahweh compared such that he can cast a shadow? The reader receives no answer. In any case, the poet turns again to Israel using the vehicles of plants and the tenor of Israel's restoration. The plants have changed. Instead of lily, poplar, and olive tree, the poet now refers to grain, vine, and wine. Unlike the earlier series, the focus has shifted to plants that have commercial value or are agricultural commodities themselves, such as wine. These cola represent the culmination of this botanical imagery, the final bounty that certain plants afford. Yet even here, the final note struck is not that of commerce but that of the memory, or even the ethereal fragrance (NRSV translates "fragrance"), of good wine.

In the final verse of this divine speech, the deity addresses Ephraim directly in a challenging voice, much as at the beginning of the chapter:

> O Ephraim, what have I to do with idols?
> It is I who answer and look after you.
> I am like an evergreen cypress;
> from me comes your fruit.*

As before, the first person address turns to simile. With yet another type of flora, the poet likens Yahweh to a tree, and in so doing explains retrospectively the source of the shade mentioned in v. 7. Moreover, just as the poet understood Yahweh to fructify Israel as dew moistens a plant (v. 5), so now Yahweh will provide food for Israel, just as this tree (the tree of life?) provides fruit for consumption.

This concluding simile ties together various elements of this series of similes and the direct discourse that interpenetrates the similes as well. Yahweh remains the ultimate source of growth. Hence, with the conclusion of the simile, Yahweh and not Israel, as in vv. 5b-7, is likened to a plant. Israel, through the technique of personification, remains a person, whether known as Israel or Ephraim. The poet treats them as a person fed by the deity, even though, through the rich symbolism of these similes, Israel had itself been likened to both plant growth and agricultural produce. In the final analysis, Yahweh is the one who provides food for growth.

In sum, similes are prominent literary devices in the Book of Hosea. The analytical vocabulary of vehicle and tenor helps us understand the basic character of similes. Moreover, there is significant variety in the ways that similes work. For example, two identical similes function quite differently depending on their respective literary contexts. Furthermore, similes, when combined with other similes, work to create meanings different from situations in which one simile stands by itself. The semantic relationships, just as with all parallelism, may be paradigmatic or syntagmatic, that is, the vehicle or tenor in one simile may substitute for the vehicle or tenor in the next simile, or the similes may build upon each other. In addition, to use the language of vehicle and tenor, the specific identity of the tenor is often remarkably ambiguous, as seen in our discussion of 13:3 and 13:7-8. Similes become effective because the vehicle may express a tenor that is not initially clear. As a result, the listener or reader is challenged to enter the world of the simile and to reflect upon one and another aspect of the tenor. Rather than a wooden device, the simile can be complex, both in its grammatic structure and in its rhetorical demands.

STANZA AND STROPHE

As demonstrated, simile is a stylistic device frequently used in Hebrew poetry. However, the importance of stanza and strophe in Hebrew poetry is much debated. Watson's encyclopedic work on Hebrew poetry deals with these terms in a chapter directly following the chapters on "metre" and parallelism. O'Connor employs the idiosyncratic terms, batches and staves, which he revitalized from other poetic studies to describe the strophes and stanzas.[15] Some discussion of strophe and stanza continues in assessments of Hebrew poetry, but it is generally conceded that stanzaic groupings do not exist.[16]

In the broader literary discussions, strophe and stanza are not particularly prominent. The *Princeton Handbook* has a two-paragraph discussion on strophe and three paragraphs on stanza. To be sure, there have been times in the history of various literatures when either strophe (the ode in classical Greek drama) or stanza (Spenser's *The Faerie Queene*) was a rhetorical device utilized by the poet. To add to the problems, the two terms are often used synonymously. This is frequently the case in discussions of Hebrew poetry. If they are distinguished, more frequently than not, one designates the stanza (stave à la O'Connor) as the larger unit, which is made up of varying numbers of strophes.

Watson uses the terms more carefully. For him, strophe is synonymous with the terms for the various colon combinations (bicolon, tricolon, and others). Stanzas are based on content and include certain stanza markers (such as the refrain). However, in the end he says, "There are no hard and fast rules which can be applied. It is, to some extent, a matter of feel."[17] Given these definitions, the term "strophe" affords little explanatory power. Moreover, if stanza is determined only by "feel," it is doubtful that the interpreter gains much precision by using the term or its equivalent. On the other hand, most agree that readers segment poems into sense units as they read. Nevertheless elements signal these sense units to the reader.

The term "stanza" is most frequently understood to be a semantic unit, that is, a unit of meaning. Some scholars have tried to identify the stanza as a grammatically or metrically regular unit. This task, of course, has been difficult with Hebrew poetry, since regularity of rhythm, number of cola combined, series of identical parallelistic strategies, and so forth, are difficult to find.[18] It is not our contention that groups beyond the bicolon or tricolon never occur, rather that stanzaic style does not appear in Hebrew poetry. Groupings occur within the constraints of parallelism, rhythm, and other stylistic devices. There are delimiters, both grammatic and semantic, that signal the reader that units external to the bicolon, or any other configuration of cola, hold lines together and separate them. However, the delimiting is not accomplished through breaking units into stanzas.

The term "stanza," even if understood not to suggest any kind of regularity, provides little leverage for the interpreter of Hebrew poetry. The term "verse paragraph," which is defined as "one or more sentences unified by a dominant mood or thought,"[19] also appears to have minimal analytical value for the understanding of Hebrew poetry. Mood and thought are problematic terms, since they are open to such diverse interpretations. It is more important to identify those grammatic and semantic elements that link and separate cola, of whatever arrangement. The delimiters found in Hebrew poetry to separate or bind various numbers of lines reside at multiple grammatic and semantic levels. Our discussions of parallelism and rhythm have already pointed to some of these devices.

Many elements signal segmentation and contiguity, but we will highlight only a few of them. There are efforts to list these elements, much as one attempts to list the types of parallelism.[20] However, to date no one has provided a comprehensive taxonomy, since the variables are so numerous. It makes far greater sense to identify sense units[21] that are held together—and reported from other sense units—by various grammatic and semantic devices.

The similes in Hosea present several examples. First, the linked similes of Hosea 13 demonstrate how the rhetorical device of the similes, coupled with the structural elements derived from the oracle of judgment, both separate and draw together the poetry. In both oracles (13:1-3 and 4-8) the indictments (vv. 1-2 and 4-6) are expressed in direct language. The similes appear in the sentences that conclude the oracles. It serves little purpose to discuss this segmentation in terms of stanzas. The fact that the sentence following the indictment in 13:7-8 is cast in similes, chiastically structured, with both paradigmatic and syntagmatic semantic development serves far better the purposes of understanding the internal and external relationships of the cola and of identifying a discrete rhetorical unit. One might even refer to these units as sense units.

The refrain and the chorus are stylistic devices that segment poems. A refrain can be formulated as an exact repetition, such as the five clauses iterated in Amos 4:6, 8, 9, 10, 11 ("yet you did not return to me, says the LORD"). Or they may vary slightly, as the refrains in the first two chapters of Amos: 1:3, 6, 9, 11, 13; 2:1, 4, 6 ("for three transgressions of . . . , I will not provoke the punishment"). The chorus of Psalm 136 in every other colon is identical ("for his steadfast love endures forever"). This repetition within the bicolon draws the reader's attention to an identity that continues from beginning to end. On the other hand, the other portion of the bicolon is constantly changing. In fact, the non-chorus segment of almost every bicola tells of a new event, yet the new event always makes the same claim, namely, that God has provided in diverse times and places for all humankind. These actions by the deity in turn deserve continuing thanksgiving.

The stylistic devices available to the Hebrew poet for delimiting and connecting larger units are, more frequently than not, detected after the reading or hearing. The first time we read or hear the refrain or chorus we do not know it is a repeated element. Only after we have seen it the second time do we begin to grasp the rhetorical significance. The so-called inclusio, or enveloping structure, in which a word or phrase or even bicolon segments a text by appearing at the beginning and at the end of a unit, further illustrates this point. Psalm 8, following the superscription, begins and ends with the same lines.

> O Yahweh, our LORD,
> how majestic is your name
> in all the earth!*

The inclusio brackets the entire psalm. Each of Psalms 145–150 begin and end with the so-called imperative colon, "Praise Yahweh." Individual bicola and tricola may commence and conclude with identical or nearly identical words, phonologic elements, or morphologic equivalents. The repetition of key words and phrases also serves to hold cola together and to segment them. The repeated "voice of Yahweh" in Ps. 29:3-9 segments the praise of Yahweh from the call to praise in vv. 1-2 and the concluding praise from the temple in vv. 10-11. The repetition of this key phrase holds together a diverse semantic and grammatic unit. The pounding sevenfold repetition of the phrase appears among nominal and verbal cola, bicola utilizing the phrase elliptically, others not using ellipsis, and similes with diverse vehicles, just to mention several stylistic devices present in this section of Psalm 29.

All of this suggests that rather than rely on stanzaic language, which often assumes some extraneous semantic or grammatic strategy, we look to multiple stylistic devices, including parallelism and rhythm, which indicate the organization of poetic lines. The purpose of our discussing briefly these stylistic features suggests the diversity of devices open to the Hebrew poet and also reminds the poetic interpreter of the interdependence of parallelism, rhythm, and numerous other stylistic devices.

5
Poetic Analysis

Our primary goal in this chapter is to examine several biblical texts from a variety of perspectives, the most important of which is consideration of the text as poetry. We are interested not simply in reading the text "as literature" but in suggesting how other critical perspectives may work together with attention to the poetic features of a biblical text. To comment on the "poetic" features of the text does not, to be sure, in some mechanical or direct way lead to understanding the meaning of a text. To ignore such features, however, impoverishes one's assessment and interpretation of the literature. In fact, a controlling metaphor or the prominence of any other literary device—for example, personification, hyperbole, or irony—may decisively affect one's interpretation of the poetic text. Such literary considerations have an important part to play in the interpretive process.

We shall consider a representative sample of various sorts of poetry found in the Hebrew Bible, including prophetic utterance (Isaiah 5), pentateuchal poem (Deuteronomy 32), and a psalm (Psalm 1). However, some important types of poetry have not been addressed, for example, lyric poetry as found in the Song of Songs and wisdom poetry as found in Job and Ecclesiastes. Nonetheless, on the basis of the work that we have included here, we hope to provide sufficient models so that the reader will be in a position to move on to an appreciation and interpretation of the full variety of Hebrew poetic texts.

When we proceed with the poetic analysis, we will not propose a specific set of "steps" to follow, since the casual reader, the person preparing to teach or preach from a Hebrew poem, or the more advanced Hebrew specialist—all of whom will be enjoying and interpreting biblical poetry for quite different purposes—will work in diverse ways. Perhaps an analogy would help. Both the amateur rock collector and the professional geologist look at a mineral crystal. The task of the geologist is, typically, quite different from that of the amateur, who is, essentially, a connoisseur. However, both need to know something about crystallography in order to appreciate a particular type of mineral crystal. Typically, the geologist will have a more detailed knowledge of such matters. However, both rock collector and geologist will have gained a better perspective on the crystal in question as a result of their knowledge. In addition, the analytical steps before the rock collector and the geologist change when they confront a different sort of mineral, such as an opal, which has no crystalline structure. The situation with various readers of Hebrew poetry is similar. One person might read a Hebrew poem to prepare an expository sermon. This task would involve a set of requirements different from reading the text for devotional purposes or for pure pleasure. Some readings of the poem may demand a very close, detailed analysis, whereas others would merely be enhanced by a rudimentary understanding of rhythm, parallelism, and other poetic techniques. All readings, however, benefit from knowledge about Hebrew poetry. Moreover, different poems place different sorts of demands upon the readers. One proverb presents one set of problems, a speech of Job another set. For these reasons, we avoid a rigid interpretive paradigm.

We do offer several preliminary comments on the ways in which the poetic analysis proceeds and constitutes a part of the larger interpretive process. First, in each instance it is important to link historical-critical concerns with more singularly literary issues so as to provide the basis for a comprehensive interpretation of the poem in question. Hence the analysis of each poem should include attention to issues, where appropriate and useful, such as philology and form criticism. We will examine such issues, which may be viewed as background or historical-critical matters, before pursuing our poetic analysis. To address those issues first does not suggest that it is necessary to create a historical setting for a poetic text in order to understand it. Rather, we work in this way in order to allow the literary analysis to benefit from other important elements in the interpretation of a particular text, for example, its form as a hymn or a lawsuit. By incorporating such information early in the interpretive process, one avoids the all-too-common risk of allowing the poem to rest in a vacuum, without appropriate contextualization (as in our earlier discussion of Alter's analysis of Isa. 24:17-20).

Second, after gaining some necessary historical-critical background about the poem and after reading the poem several times in order to gain an idea of its basic content, the reader should attempt to discern the most prominent poetic features in the text. Sometimes one element may stand out, for example, semantic parallelism or the use of irony. We have, in fact, been impressed by the frequency with which one, or perhaps two, poetic devices stand out in a given poem. At other times several special features may appear without any of them achieving prominence. However, when some element does appear prominently, it is worthy of attention at the outset of the poetic analysis. For example, if rhythmic variety between bicola or tricola seems especially prominent or if personification occurs with unusual regularity, then these features should be noted early in the interpretive process.

One should not stop with the dominant or most obvious features; rather, one should be attentive to others as well. For example, if one poetic device, such as parallelism, has been the dominant feature that attracted attention, then it is appropriate to turn to the other basic categories, rhythm or various tropes, to ensure a complete assessment of the poem. At this point, one should both note the presence of other devices and attempt to discern whether they work consistently with the dominant poetic device. Only after these tasks have been accomplished is it possible to draw some tentative conclusions about the character and meaning of the poem.

A word of caution is appropriate regarding the task of discerning rhythm and rhythmic patterns in Hebrew poetry. The non-Hebrew reader is at a distinct disadvantage when attempting to make observations about rhythm in the Hebrew text. No translation can fully preserve the rhythm of the original language. In the three examples provided below, we have given some clues about the presence of the "original" rhythm whether in the mode of transliteration or translation.

DEUTERONOMY 32

The poems embedded in the Pentateuch are like gemstones that occur in a rough matrix. To say this is not to demean pentateuchal narrative or legal material, the predominant pentateuchal matrix. It is, however, to recognize that these poems have an almost crystalline appearance when compared with their surroundings. The language of these poems is dense; they are much more terse than other pentateuchal texts. Most of these poems are, by scholarly consensus, deemed to be much older than the narratives in which they are situated. In fact, they may well comprise some of the oldest literature preserved in the Old Testament. For this reason alone, these poems deserve special treatment; and they have received it. As particularly ancient verse, they may well offer unique data about both ancient Hebrew poetry and ancient Israelite religion. In addition, because they are especially old, these poems present linguistic peculiarities. Hence, considerable scholarly attention has been devoted to poems such as Exodus 15 and Deuteronomy 33. The Song of Moses (Deuteronomy 32) has received less attention, despite its obvious literary sophistication.[1]

Deuteronomy 32, often known as the Song of Moses, is a long poem, comprising forty-three verses. The Book of Deuteronomy set it, through the introduction in Deut. 31:30, as a libretto spoken by Moses to the people assembled on the Plains of Moab. The poem does not sit easily in its context, since these verses involve not only a reprise of Israel's early history with Yahweh but also an indictment of Israel for religious apostasy once the people were in the land. As a result, Yahweh acts punitively against his people (32:19-25). The final portion of the poem, at least vv. 31-43, functions as a critique of other nations, a vindication of Israel, and a paean to Yahweh.

Scholars who have devoted attention to Deuteronomy 32 have, for the most part, dealt with detailed philological problems. Broader questions about date of composition and literary form have received less treatment. There is, in fact, no scholarly consensus about the date of composition. To be sure, there is almost unanimous scholarly judgment that Moses is not the author of the piece. The "Israel" described in the poem is clearly an Israel that has lived in the promised land, long after the death of Moses. How long, though, is something of a problem. On the basis of a philological study, W. F. Albright proposed a date for "a written original not later than the tenth century B.C."[2] G. E. Wright tentatively placed the poem one century later, during the reign of Jehoahaz, more particularly, ca. 815–805 B.C.E.[3] For some scholars, it is possible to date the text to the early monarchic period. On the other hand, since an imminent demise of the nation seems apparent and since the sorts of indictments made by Jeremiah also appear in Deuteronomy 32, it has not been uncommon to date the poem to the late seventh century or even sixth century B.C.E.[4]

Attempts to date the poem have not been particularly successful, but there has been a stronger, though certainly not unanimous, consensus about the poem's literary form. Wright argued that the genre of the *rib* or covenant lawsuit provided the fundamental structure of Deuteronomy 32. Standard features of this genre, following the analysis of H. B. Huffmon,[5] include:

I. A description of the scene of judgment
II. The speech of the plaintiff
    A. Heaven and earth appointed as judges
    B. Summons to the defendant (or judges)
    C. Address in the second person to the defendant
        1. Accusation of the defendant in question form
        2. Refutation of the defendant's possible arguments
        3. Specific indictment

Wright argued that some, though not all, of these features are present in Deuteronomy 32.[6] However, his version of the basic form is simpler: call to the witnesses to give ear to the proceedings, introductory statement of the case at issue by the divine judge and prosecutor or by his earthly official, recital of the benevolent acts of the deity, the indictment, and the sentence. In terms of these categories, v. 1 represents a form of the call to the witnesses, here heaven and earth. However, the poem includes more than that described by these standard rubrics, namely, expansions in vv. 2 and 30-43. Verse 2 allows the speaker to function in the role of a wisdom teacher, whereas vv. 39-42 draw on holy war hymnic material to elaborate upon the character of the deity's judgmental actions. Wright's claim is not so much that an original poem was expanded but that the basic or pristine form of the covenant lawsuit had been elaborated in this particular poem. In any case, form critical analysis provides an insight fundamental to any literary analysis of this text, namely, that it follows certain formal conventions known in ancient Israel. The genre of the covenant lawsuit helps provide a context in which to understand the poetic text. To say this is not to suppose that this poem is simply another example of a well-known form, but it is to state that the basic form of the lawsuit— call to the witnesses, statement of the case, recitation of past history, indictment, and sentence—will either be present in the text or its absence will be significant.

Because Deuteronomy 32 is such a long poem, our treatment must of necessity be suggestive rather than exhaustive. As a result, we will devote our attention to vv. 1-3, 10-14, and 39-42. We focus on these verses for particular reasons. They include not only some of the most

figurative language in the chapter but also what Wright argued was the
earliest poem, vv. 1, 3, 10-14, and expansionary material, vv. 2, 39-
42. Our choice of verses is not intended to argue for or against the
original unity of the poem. Rather, this choice of verses allows us to
assess the greatest variety attested in the poem.

> Give ear, O heavens, and I will speak;
>   let the earth hear the words of my mouth.
> May my teaching drop like the rain,
>   my speech condense like the dew;
> like gentle rain on grass,
>   like showers on new growth.
> For I will proclaim the name of the LORD;
>   ascribe greatness to our God!
>
> Deut. 32:1-3

The poem begins in the imperative mood. Moses, the speaker
(Deut. 31:30), addresses, somewhat surprisingly, not the people but
the heavens and the earth. The moods of the verbs are subtly nuanced,
as is apparent even in English translation. The first verb, "give ear," is
a second person imperative, literally, "you give ear," whereas the second verb is couched in the third person imperative, often called jussive or indirect imperative, "let hear." Whereas the heavens are addressed directly, "listen," the earth, the domain of humanity, is not.
There is, therefore, an initial emphasis on the rhetorical primacy of
the heavens. They are addressed first and directly; the place where
humans dwell is addressed second and indirectly.

In addition, the first colon, a three-accent line (as is the second
colon), includes a purpose clause. When the heavens give ear, then
Moses will speak, that is, Moses' speaking is a result of the heavens'
readiness to give ear. This logical connection included in the purpose
clause does not recur in the second line, nor is it presumed. The earth
will simply hear the words of the speaker. In fact, the second colon
does provide new information, namely, what precisely it is that the
heavens and the earth will hear: "the words of my mouth" from a
speaker other than deity.

In this first verse, what might be viewed as synonymous parallelism
is considerably more complex than that label would suggest:

> Give ear, O heavens, and I will speak;
>   let the earth hear the words of my mouth.

70

There is morphological variety in the verbs: "give ear" is an imperative, "let hear" is a jussive or indirect imperative. There is syntactic variety: vocative and purpose clause in the first colon, double object in the second colon. And there is semantic variety, as we have suggested in the previous paragraph. However, the rhythmic pattern of two lines of three accents each provides a consistent structure. In this one verse, we have present the two contrasting elements constitutive of Hebrew poetry, namely, regularity and variety.

Subtly linking the next bicolon with the foregoing is another indirect imperative verb, "may drop." However, now the speaker addresses himself in something akin to a soliloquy: "May my teaching drop like the rain, my speech condense like the dew." Although imperative discourse continues, an entirely new vocabulary and set of imagery has been introduced, that of fructive water and fertility. Moreover, it is imagery consistent with that of the "geography," namely, reference to heavens and earth, adduced in the first verse. The knowledge/teaching of the speaker will proceed down, from heaven to earth, just as does the rain. Reference to heaven and earth in the first verse creates the imagery of descent that controls the verticality expressed in the second verse.

At this point the poet introduces a simile to develop his point. The water imagery is explored with full semantic variety—four different nouns are used for various forms of water: rain (*māṭār*), dew (*ṭal*), torrent (*śāʿîr*), and showers (*rĕbîbîm*). Hence a translation such as NRSV is insufficient. Rather than providing a picture of gentle drizzle wetting a lawn, the Hebrew text creates a picture of a torrent laying down standing grass. The rain is, to be sure, fructive. However, it is also powerful, a driving force. The emphasis here does not lie on the fertility engendered by the rain, although that connotation cannot be denied. Instead, the preposition "upon," repeated in both lines of the simile, stresses that the rain will land on or against something, not simply that it will make something green.

The NRSV's translation "grass" and "new growth" is also misleading; one could translate "grass" and "turf"; so NJB. Both nouns are to be understood simply as referring to green vegetation, without any special connotation regarding tenderness or size. Clearly the biblical writer is focusing here not on the sorts of greenery engendered but on the life-giving character of the moisture. This distinctive feature of the simile, with its focus on rain as both life-engendering and powerful, is underlined by the rhythmic pattern that undergirds it, one different from the foregoing cola. Here the author uses a two-accent bicolon to turn his phrase instead of the earlier three-accent bicola. Rhythm emphasizes the distinctive trope, a simile, employed at this point in the poem.

With v. 3 the author returns to the more direct language of the first verse. He introduces it with an emphatic particle, which may well stand apart from the rhythmic pattern of a three-accent bicolon, that is, anacrusis (involves a word that stands outside the normal rhythmic pattern). "Indeed, the name of Yahweh will I proclaim" insists, by dint of its word order, that the name of Yahweh has pride of place. These are the first of the "words of my mouth" that the author offers. The second line of the bicolon differs fundamentally, both in its grammatical structure and in its semantics. Whereas the first line reported what it was that the speaker/author would do, the second line returns to the second person imperative language of the first line in v. 1, creating a grammatical envelope, or inclusio. Moreover, the presence of the inclusio emphasizes that one section of the entire poem has been completed. This is also corroborated by a form-critical assessment of the poem, namely, that the initial summons of the witnesses has been completed. With this final bicolon, the reader learns that the subject of the poet's address involves the deity, more particularly the invocation of his name and greatness.

Despite the formal integrity of this introduction to the poem, there is a semantic force driving the reader beyond the boundaries of this section. The reason for one to heed the imperative rhetoric has yet to be provided. To be sure, the poet has reported that one reason the heavens and earth should pay heed is that Moses will speak. However, that rationale does not explain why it is that those who hear the poem should "ascribe greatness to our God." The reason is provided in the next section of the poem. God should be praised because he is "the Rock," because "his work is perfect," because "all his ways are just," and because he is "a faithful God, without deceit; just and upright is he." For all those reasons one is to ascribe greatness to Yahweh. This semantic link between the first and second sections of the poem is underlined rhythmically. Both vv. 3 and 4a are cast in a three-accent rhythmic pattern, thereby linking by stress what is also linked by content. In sum, although one section has ended, the semantics of the first section push the reader on within the poem.

We turn now to vv. 10-14:

72

> He sustained him in a desert land,
>> in a howling wilderness waste;
> he shielded him, cared for him,
>> guarded him as the apple of his eye.
> As an eagle stirs up its nest,
>> and hovers over its young;
> as it spreads its wings, takes them up,
>> and bears them aloft on its pinions,
> the LORD alone guided him;
>> no foreign god was with him.
> He set him atop the heights of the land,
>> and fed him with produce of the field;
> he nursed him with honey from the crags,
>> with oil from flinty rock;
> curds from the herd, and milk from the flock,
>> with fat of lambs and rams;
> Bashan bulls and goats,
>> together with the choicest wheat—
>> you drank fine wine from the blood of grapes.
>
> Deut. 32:10-14

In these verses the audience is different from that in the foregoing verses. Verse 6 requires that "his degenerate children" (v. 5), a filial image for Yahweh's people, be those queried and addressed, that is, the heavens and the earth are no longer the object of address. After a brief interrogation and admonition (vv. 6-9), the poem continues with a highly imagistic depiction of Yahweh's early relation with Israel. Verse 10 commences with reference to Yahweh's initial action toward Israel and to the physical setting of that activity. Although we think v. 10 provides the beginning of another major section of the poem, this verse develops grammatically out of the verses that precede it. "He sustained him," one Hebrew word with which the verse begins, includes two pronouns, the object and subject of the verb. Only the action described in vv. 8-9 makes clear who these parties are, namely, Yahweh, the subject, finding Jacob-Israel, the object. The situation is complex, since the word "father" is used (vv. 6 and 7) to describe two different figures: in v. 6, God; in v. 7, a human parent.

This version of Israel's early experience with Yahweh begins in fairly neutral terms: "he sustained him in a desert land." The sentence is balanced exactly, at least in the number of syllables that occur in the next colon. However, the syntax of the cola is in no way identical. The first complete sentence is balanced by a phrase that describes one aspect of the wilderness. The phrase "desert land" is general, creating an image of an uncultivated, non-urban place. For the purposes of this poem, the choice of *midbār* is appropriate, since it is one of the nouns used to describe the place of the so-called wilderness wanderings. It is that place in which Israel was found (so Hebrew text), a place that involves both geography, that is, a Sinai sort of wasteland, and history, a time after the exodus but before the entry into the land. However, the balancing phrase says more and says it differently. The second colon is made up of three nouns in a series, all of which modify each other, a complex case of nominal hendiadys: *tōhû* ("wasteland"), *yĕlēl* ("howling"), and *yĕšimōn* ("wilderness"). Two of these words might be expected. *Yĕšimōn* is regularly used to balance *midbār*, so Pss. 78:40; 106:14, cases in which both nouns refer to the place where the wilderness wanderings took place. And *tōhû* normally refers to untracked wilderness (Job 6:18; 12:24), without special reference to the place of the wilderness wandering. The truly innovative claim is that such wilderness is noisy, that is, that it can be termed a place of howling. Are we to understand this phrase to mean that the place is personified, as a person or an animal that howls, or that it is a place of howling sounds (e.g., noisy wind)? Although the text is ambiguous, this particular triliteral stem, *yll*, when used as a verb, normally occurs either with humans or animals as the subject. As a result, the poet in all likelihood was suggesting that the wilderness itself howls, a truly remarkable image in which wasteland is personified.

In this noisy, trackless waste, Yahweh finds someone who is lost, perhaps a child, were one to infer age from the simile of v. 11. If the initial bicolon of v. 10 is essentially descriptive, that is, providing nouns that depict the place where Israel was found, the next bicolon highlights verbs, which describe the action of the deity. Three of the five words in this bicolon are verbs; the other two words, which make up a simile, serve to modify the action described. The contrast between the lines involves a contrast between place and action, a contrast enhanced by the diverse morphology of noun and verb. Alliteration is prominent in the first colon, *yĕsōbĕbenhû yĕbônĕnēhû*, a colon that presents two imperfect verbs with third person masculine singular suffixes: "he shielded him, he cared for him." These two morphologically similar verbs describe essentially similar action, namely, action between two agents, the deity and the child whom he has found. The final colon of the verse, although rhythmically balanced with the foregoing colon, is decidedly different. It does begin with another imperfect verb, the third in a row, but it is followed by a graphic (and well known in mistranslation, "the apple of his eye") simile, the whole of which should be translated, "he protected him as he would the pupil of his eye." Not only is the grammar different, including a prepositional phrase in the last colon, but a new connotation is established in this final line. One guards or protects an eye from someone or something, a speck of dirt in or an enemy assault on the eye. In the foregoing colon, the author described the singular action of the deity toward the foundling. Now that action involves something beyond the two parties. This development in thought is echoed by the "progression" in the syntax, two verbs in the first colon and one verb modified by a prepositional phrase in the second colon. Perhaps it is not too much to speak of two aspects of a parental image: lovingly holding and protecting a child.[7]

The pattern of creative poetic juxtaposition continues in the next colon, which begins with yet another simile, one that develops the connotation of parental activity, which had been established subtly in the previous verse. Here the deity is likened first to an eagle that bestirs the young in its nest, presumably enabling them to learn to fly, and then to an eagle that hovers over its young. In these two similes the reader is introduced to a regal bird, swift in flight (2 Sam. 1:23; the bird is often used in comparisons with humans, especially in military contexts, Deut. 28:49; Jer. 48:40; 49:22). According to Exod. 19:4, Yahweh may be likened to the eagle, in that instance a reference to his lifting up of Israelite slaves and bringing them to him. The notion of an elegant and swift bird of prey is not as prominent in Deut. 32:11 as is the image of the bird as dutiful and powerful parent. On the one hand, the eagle stimulates its young to develop properly; on the other hand, the eagle protects its young when they are in the nest. One aspect of this image that we find particularly interesting involves the multiple nestlings. Whereas the initial reference in this part of the poem is to Jacob as a single foundling, and whereas again in vv. 12-13 the object of Yahweh's mercies is a sole individual, here in v. 11a, the object of Yahweh's mercies are nestlings. This constitutes a creative attempt to recognize that the object of Yahweh's attention is, at one and the same time, a someone, Jacob, and a group, Israelites.

In the second part of the verse, which almost becomes a narrative, the poet continues in the simile but reverts to referring to an individual rather than to nestlings (cf. NRSV). Moreover, there appears to be a sequence of action: the eagle spreads its wings, he takes him (presumably one nestling), and he bears him up on his pinions. The image is of a powerful raptor acting in the interest of its young. However, the goal of the bird's action is unclear. Where is the eaglet being taken—to safety, to eat, or to a place to practice flying? The reader is not told. The poet has focused on the singular and powerful action of the bird, not on the immediate goal of its activity.[8]

This eagle simile in v. 11 portrays one dominant image of the deity and his action. As befits such stylistic consistency of focus, the poetry has cast the lines in a decidedly balanced fashion: two lines of seven syllables each and two lines of nine and eight syllables respectively. It is interesting that the weightier colon, v. 11b, conveys weighty action, the eagle bearing up one of its young in flight. Here again, rhythm complements semantic elements in the poem.

Verse 12 marks a decisive shift, semantically, syntactically, and rhythmically, from the foregoing symbolism. The cola are shorter. Instead of nine syllables as in the fourth colon in v. 11, the first colon of v. 12 includes seven syllables, balanced by seven syllables in the second colon. The poet shifts back to language concerning Yahweh and the object of his affection and attention, for example, "the LORD led him." The bicolon commences with a disjunctive clause, one in which a non-verb occurs first: "Yahweh alone led him." Once outside the imagery of nestlings, there is no problem in referring to a lone individual. It is almost as if the author has returned to the language with which this section of the poem began, namely, that of v. 10a. In equally straightforward language, the poet comments on what is missing in this desert entourage, a foreign god. There is some ambiguity in this colon, which states, "there was no foreign god with him." Who is the "him," the foundling or Yahweh? Most have assumed the former, namely, the foundling at that point was religiously acceptable, not going after foreign gods. However, the situation might not be so simple. Would one naturally think of someone lost, someone requiring assistance, one who is a lost child, as someone accompanied by a foreign god? Perhaps not. Alternately, the claim may be that the youth simply did not have the sorts of votive deities referred to in Gen. 35:2. In either case, it would appear that the standard charge of apostasy is not at work in this part of the poem, since going after foreign gods is something Israelite authors normally associate with life in the land (cf. Deut. 31:10; Jer. 5:19). But could one sensibly think about Yahweh as accompanied by a foreign god? If one appeals to language about Yahweh having a spouse, for example, Asherah at Kuntillet ʿAjrud,[9] then perhaps the poet is indeed referring to Yahweh's helpful action without any assistance. After all, the image of Yahweh as a parental eagle could imply another parent. However, in balance, we accept the first option, since it allows for the possibility of poetic foreshadowing, namely, an ability later in the poem to refer to a time during which Israel will be accompanied by a foreign god. (This is the situation described in vv. 16-17.) In any case, the pair, Yahweh and the lost person, are alone. Yahweh is the sole deity in the scene. And this affirmation serves to punctuate this poet's description of Yahweh's first encounter with Israel.

In vv. 13-14, the poet returns to the notion of what Yahweh has done on behalf of the individual whom he has found. In six of these seven cola, there is a consistent theme, the marvelous diet provided for the foundling by Yahweh. However, the first colon of v. 13 begins with a claim not having to do with food. Instead, the author continues with the motif of Yahweh providing the source of movement for the foundling, so vv. 11-12. But the imagery is now different: "he set him atop the heights of the land." The notion is unusual. The Hebrew phrase *rkb ʿal* is typically used to describe someone riding an animal. Here, however, "the heights of the land" symbolizes the steed upon which the individual is mounted.[10] Presumably, the individual, if mounted on the heights, has a vantage point that enables him to survey the countryside. It is an almost godlike vantage—Micah 1:3 refers to the deity coming down and walking on "the heights of the earth." What the deity does in Micah 1:3, that is, walk on mountains, is not radically dissimilar from that which he helps the individual to do here, namely, ride on the mountains. The foundling here becomes nearly divine in ability and perspective. It is interesting that this notion is conveyed in a colon of unusual length, ten syllables, and is therefore set off from the second and ensuing cola.

Such godlike abilities are almost necessary, given the eating and drinking that Jacob confronts. It is not the diet that is so peculiar as it is the variety and source of the foodstuffs. Not only field and flock but even a rock produces that which is to be consumed. As a result, there is a hyperbolic tone: the riding of mountains and eating honey from a rock. Distinctive words enhance the miraculous character of that which is being provided. Not only does the person eat a fantastic variety of food, the individual has the best of things to eat: the best (*ḥēleb*) of the wheat and the best (*ḥēleb*) of the lambs (v. 14). It is interesting that the morphology of the words in these balanced lines emphasizes the peculiar abundance of these goods. In v. 14, in all but the last colon, there are no verbs. Instead, the author piles up noun after noun to emphasize the incredible variety of foodstuffs. However, there is not a strong balance in the rhythm, since the syllable count varies from four syllables, for example, the first colon of v. 14, to eleven syllables, for example, the third colon of v. 14. One senses that the poet has provided rhythmic variety to balance the semantic and morphological similarity.

This section of the poem ends on a note of exaggerated bounty and consumption and foreshadows the result of such overconsumption, namely, someone growing fat (v. 15). What might be taken as a comment on the agricultural bounty that Yahweh provides involves a negative potential, which manifests itself later in the poem.

We move on, however, past the condemnation of a bloated Jeshurun, his punishment, and then some positive action of the deity on behalf of his people, to virtual hymnic language (vv. 39-43) at the end of the poem:

> See now that I, even I, am he;
>   there is no god beside me.
> I kill and I make alive;
>   I wound and I heal;
>   and no one can deliver from my hand.
> For I lift up my hand to heaven,
>   and swear: As I live forever,
> when I whet my flashing sword,
>   and my hand takes hold on judgment;
> I will take vengeance on my adversaries,
>   and will repay those who hate me.
> I will make my arrows drunk with blood,
>   and my sword shall devour flesh—
> with the blood of the slain and the captives,
>   from the long-haired enemy.
>
> Praise, O heavens, his people,
>   worship him, all you gods!
> For he will avenge the blood of his children,
>   and take vengeance on his adversaries;
> he will repay those who hate him,
>   and cleanse the land for his people.
>   Deut. 32:39-43

The rhythm with which this section begins is complex. One can view the first nine words as two cola or possibly as three: "See now, indeed; I, I am he; there is no god except me" or, as with NRSV, "See now that I, even I, am he." Given the prominence of cola with three accents throughout the remainder of the poem, we incline to the former option. Hence this portion of the poem commences with one tricolon, which is replete with personal pronouns, four of them, all of which refer to the deity. Here the poet utilizes morphology, the prominence of pronouns, to focus on the singularity of Yahweh. Such morphological regularity produces a striking prominence of the long "i" vowel, which signals the first person in classical Hebrew grammar. As a result, there is strong phonetic consistency as well. However, this action of the deity produces a general assertion. Hence there follows another tricolon, which provides the reasons to accept Yahweh's singularity. Again morphology provides an interpretive key. Verbs are uniquely prominent: "*I* slay, I bring to life; I injure, and *I* heal." The "I's" that are in italics represent independent personal pronouns, whereas those not in italics are part of the verbal structure. The italicized independent personal pronouns provide an envelope for the four verbs that define the range of Yahweh's activity and that sustain the notion that only he is God. Moreover, in terms of semantics, the author is using the device of antithesis to make his case. Not only can Yahweh do difficult things, he can do antithetically difficult things, unexpectedly different things. For example, a human can slay, but only a deity can bring to life. Moreover, if one human kills another, one does not expect the slayer even to attempt to heal, much less to revivify the corpse. Such impossible, unexpected things are possible only with Yahweh. To provide closure for this unit, the poet returns to the 'ên (negative) particle, which occurred at the end of the first tricolon, and strikes a negative note, namely, that once someone is in Yahweh's grasp, no one can provide rescue.

The two initial tricola (v. 39) are followed by a bicolon (v. 40) with much longer balanced lines (nine and eleven syllables respectively). Although the first person language continues, a new semantic element is introduced in this bicolon. To be sure, the motif of the deity's hand continues. However, it figures in a new context: "For I lift my hand to the heaven, and swear, 'As I live forever'"(v. 40). This weighty bicolon introduces an oath uttered by Yahweh. The very density of the colon underlines the gravity of the oath. The poet then moves on to the content of the oath: "if I draw my shiny sword, and my hand seizes justice."* Here the language is metaphoric. We know what it is to draw a sword; to grasp justice is, however, puzzling. At least this much is clear, namely, that mišpāṭ, "justice," can here function symbolically as a weapon. Those who violate justice will be slain by the weapon of justice. This particular metaphor points to Yahweh as a warrior-avenger, one who is just (cf. v. 4) and not simply involved in atavistic bloodshed.

The oath continues with fairly traditional language in the second colon of v. 41. In that bicolon the author, however, personalizes the enemy by describing them as those who hate Yahweh. In v. 42, the poet moves on to the means by which Yahweh will take vengeance. The poet utilizes the technique of personification, that is, speaking of arrows that become drunk and a sword that devours. That which humans may do—become drunk and devour—provides a means by which to describe the action of Yahweh's weapons.

Verbal morphology marks off v. 43 as distinct, a conclusion to the poem. The imperative verbs here mirror the mood of those in v. 1 of the poem. There is, however, a significant change. In v. 1, the heavens and the earth were being addressed. We might expect that the song would end with Israel's praise of the deity. Such is not the case. Rather, the nations are the objects of these imperative verbs. Furthermore, they are not to praise God but instead are to praise "his people." Given the virile capacities of Jacob earlier in the poem, such praise is, per-haps, not surprising. Nonetheless, the reasons for this praise border on the ironic. The nations are to sing praise because of what Yahweh does to the enemies of his people, namely, to other nations. Such praise becomes a parody of praise, since it involves the defeat of at least some of those who sing praise. The parodic praise is summarized by an inclusio that unites the final two bicola of the poem, an inclusio established by the word 'ammô, "his people," in the first and last lines of v. 43.

Since we have not examined all of Deuteronomy 32, it would be inappropriate to comment on the entire poem. It does seem clear, however, that attention to verb morphology, rhythm, symbolic lan-guage, personification, and foreshadowing assist in the interpretation of the poem. Moreover, attention to Deuteronomy 32 as poetry does not involve the creation of a simple catalog of poetic techniques. Rather, for example, the subtle transition from the notion of plenty and satiety to dull fatness, vv. 13-15, addresses a theme critical to the poem, namely, the relation between Yahweh's blessings and curses on Israel. To make these assessments is to supplement but not to replace other ways of viewing this poem, that is, from form-critical or philological perspectives. Not to undertake such literary analysis, however, risks a reading that fails to appreciate and understand this poem.

ISAIAH 5:1-7

Our second example of biblical poetry is taken from the book of Isaiah. Isaiah 5:1-7 provides an interesting text, since it, unlike many other units in the prophetic corpus, makes up a complete poem that may be isolated from the surrounding verses. The prose verses with strong eschatological coloration that precede it, Isa. 4:2-6, and the woe oracles that follow it, Isa 5:8-30, set off the song about a vineyard as a distinct unit. Furthermore, Isa. 5:1-7, at least initially, appears to be a coherent poem, not a fragment or an anthology.[11]

We ask initially two sorts of higher-critical questions before proceeding to an examination of this text as poetry. First, may the poem be dated? A related question involves our ability to attribute the poem to Isaiah ben Amoz. Was it, in all likelihood, written by this prophet who was active in the last half of the eighth century, or was it penned by those who contributed, over a period of at least two centuries, to the growth of the book of Isaiah? About a poem such as Isa. 2:2-4, there might be some debate. However, there is minimal evidence to deny Isa. 5:1-7 either to Isaiah ben Amoz or to the time in which he lived.[12] Isaiah directed much of his rhetoric to Judah and Jerusalem, which are the subjects of this poem. Further, the marks of late additions to Isaiah ben Amoz's sayings, which may include specific attention to Assyria (10:5-11; 31:1-9) or eschatological material, for example, the aforementioned Isa. 4:2-6, are not in evidence here.[13] In sum, we conclude that Isa. 5:1-7 represents the work of Isaiah ben Amoz. However, since specific historical allusions are absent, a more precise dating than the latter half of the eighth century B.C.E. is impossible.[14] If the poem may be dated to this general period, it was written in a time soon after the demise of the Northern Kingdom in 721 B.C.E. and soon before the threat posed to Judah by the neo-Assyrian empire under its emperor, Sennacherib. Hence language of destruction, as that appears in vv. 5-6, would naturally have been understood by the author and his audience within the context of the military action that Israel had experienced and that Judah would soon experience.

Second, what is the genre of this poem? There is no scholarly consensus about the answer to this question despite the fact that there have been many proposals. In 1977, J. Willis provided a convenient catalog of these proposals: "an uncle's song, a satirical polemic against Palestinian fertility cults, the prophet's song concerning his own vineyard, the prophet's song expressing sympathy for his friend Yahweh, a drinking song, a bride's love song, a groom's love song, a song of the friend to the bridegroom, a lawsuit or accusation, a fable, an allegory, and a parable."[15] J. William Whedbee deems it a juridical parable.[16] Clearly, there is a welter from among which to choose, so much so that we do not think it possible to select one or another of these labels as *the* way in which to construe the poem. Rather, we think that the notion of *Mischgattung,* a genre appropriating a number of different elements, is the best way to think about Isa. 5:1-7. Song, introduction to song, statement of judgment using curse language, and allegorical elements seem undeniably present. As a result, we approach the task of literary assessment and interpretation with a preliminary judgment that Isa. 5:1-7 comprises no single genre but is instead a poem that represents a poet's appropriation of various stylistic features attested elsewhere in ancient Israel's literature.

We may now move to a detailed examination of the poem. Isa. 5:1a would appear to be an introduction (or part thereof), not only to the poem, but to whatever song is embedded in it. Introductions typically help set the context and clarify that which follows. Not so here. This introduction is ambiguous in several ways. First, we are not told who is "singing," and the identity of "my beloved" is not revealed. Second, the noun *dôd,* which has traditionally been translated "beloved," could as well mean "uncle" or "friend," or possibly it could be the proper name of a deity. Third, the Hebrew is difficult to translate. For example, RSV renders it:

> Let me sing for my beloved
> a love song concerning his vineyard:

whereas NRSV reads:

> Let me sing for my beloved
> my love-song concerning his vineyard.

The difference between the two translations in the second colon is consequential. On the one hand, one can, with RSV, construe there to be a song, which may be characterized as a love song. Presumably it is a song authored by the songstress, a song that begins in v. 1b and is characterized by concern for the lover's experience with his vineyard. On the other hand, following NRSV, which in our judgment is a more accurate rendition of the Hebrew text,[17] the song is written by the loved one, something he sang, at least in the first instance. If this is the case, then the song does not begin until v. 3, the first place in the poem at which the male lover speaks. According to this reading, Isa. 5:1-2, and not simply v. 1a, comprises the introduction to the song. This introduction provides the mundane background necessary for us to understand the song that the beloved one, the farmer, sings.

If the beloved's song begins in v. 3, then one must recognize that the singer herself (though the singer probably refers to the prophet— here the ambiguity involves gender) is singing a song in vv. 1-2 (and v. 7). Put another way, the poet presents us with a song surrounded by a song. The song of the singer surrounds the song of the beloved, an apt image for the words of lovers. Unlike the dialogic love poetry in the Song of Songs, we have here one lover's song—though not a love song—interpreting and enveloping the song of her lover.

In Isa 5:1a, one verb controls the bicolon, "let me sing." This cohortative or indirect imperative verb sets a forceful tone, which might be better captured by the translation, "I *will* sing." The verb does not involve a request for permission to sing. Rather, it suggests the necessity for presentation of the two songs that make up this poem.

The introduction to the poem, vv. 1-2, is made up of two quite different elements. The first element, the bicolon of v. 1a, indicates the nature of the relationship between farmer and singer, namely, that of love. Further, it indicates what the primary subject matter will be: the farmer's vineyard. The rhythm is balanced symmetrically, whether one counts accents (three in each colon) or syllables (seven in each colon). This balance is enhanced by the lexical reinforcement within the two cola, "sing"//"song," "my beloved"//"my love," as well as the more general phonetic parallelism found in the prominence of "i" vowels.

The second element in the introduction is a brief narrative, vv. 1b-2.[18] In this section, one discerns a change in rhythmic structure. Instead of symmetric balance, there is a pattern of bicola in which the first line is often longer than the second (some would discern the so-called qinah meter [3 + 2]). This lack of balance anticipates the unexpected conclusion in this short narrative prologue to the farmer's song. There is an initial colon, which tells us something we already

know, namely, that the lover has a vineyard, and which tells us something that we did not know, namely, that it lay on a fertile hillock.
Lexical parallelism and phonetic parallelism link the two introductory
portions of the poem. The apparent stability of vineyard on this location is reinforced by the wordplay *kerem* ("vineyard") and *qeren*
("hill"), each word standing at the beginning of the colon in which it
occurs.

The story (v. 2) commences with a series of three long verbs, long
in the sense that the Hebrew words include both subject, verb and
object, in the form of pronominal subject. This morphological similarity creates phonetic echoing as well: *wayʿazzĕqēhû waysaqqĕlēhû
wayyiṭṭāʿēhû*. The poet continues by delineating the sorts of prepara-
tion that the beloved viticulturist has undertaken. He not only cleared,
cultivated, and planted; he has also built a tower, which is itself ambiguous (was it a tower from which to guard against theft of crop or
simply a place in which to store implements or in which to rest?) and
created a wine reservoir. The last in the series of six verbs, which
depict the work of this farmer, represents a surcease of activity: "he
expected . . ." We are left with a picture of the farmer waiting, antici-
pating a harvest of luscious grapes. Then, in the final colon, which is
the shortest in the introductory narrative, we are told about the harvest: the vineyard produced foul fruit. With that conclusion, the introductory poetic narrative ends. The poet has set the context for the
song, which is embedded in the larger poem and which follows in
vv. 3-6.

The song itself, namely, the song sung by the farmer about his vineyard, occurs in vv. 3-6. After the series of verbs in the introductory
narrative, verbs that initiated all of the bicola in that section, the poet
provides a significant break in the syntax. The particle *weʿattāh*, "and
now," begins a disjunctive clause, the sort of clause that marks a break
in the discourse. Here it signifies the beginning of a new section in the
poem, namely, the beginning of the song itself. If the verb in v. 1a
marked indirect address, the initial bicolon of the farmer's song marks
a direct imperative. In contrast to v. 1a, which is addressed to an in-
definite audience, presumably the readers of the prophetic book, the
song of vv. 3-6 focuses on a particular group, which is defined in the
initial bicolon: "inhabitants of Jerusalem//people of Judah." This colon
is a classic example of what has been called synonymous parallelism.
However, the contrast between Jerusalem-Judah and the difference
between the nouns, inhabitants-people (here a singular collective

noun), suggest that no simple synonymity is involved. The poet moves in the second colon to a larger geographic entity, the territory of Judah, while at the same time shifting to a collective noun, "people," instead of "inhabitants." In so doing, the author balances the number and the scope of the two entities involved, people and place.

The vocative address of the "beloved's song" continues with the direct imperative, "judge!" the language used in Israel's judicial assemblies (cf. Isa. 1:17, "judge/defend (the case of) the orphan"). These first bicola constitute a performative utterance, namely, in calling for Judah/Jerusalem to judge, the speaker has created a legal assembly. The singer functions as plaintiff, uttering words on his behalf and against the vineyard, which is a peculiar defendant. To have a field function as defendant is a creative literary ploy, an implicit personification. Although there is ancient Near Eastern legal precedent for charging a field animal with violence, we are unaware that a field can be so indicted.

The legal logic of v. 4 is interesting. It is not an indictment. The farmer seeks to create a defense so that he will not be blamed for the rotten produce in his vineyard. The speaker sets his defense in the interrogative mood in a very creative way. Rather than make direct reports about all that he did on behalf of the vineyard, the farmer invokes those in the assembly, the inhabitants of Jerusalem and the people of Judah, to answer his questions. There are two questions that appear to be similar. Or put another way, it would not be surprising to hear someone claim that the questions are formulated using synonymous parallelism. The questions work quite differently, however. The apparent syntactic similarity stands in contrast with semantic diversity. In answer to the first question, one expects those in the assembly to respond: "There was nothing more that you could have done." Although no answer appears after the first question, the purport of what those in the legal assembly might have said is clear. The members of the assembly presumably know what the farmer has done in and for his vineyard. Hence there was an obvious, though implicit, response. Not so with the second question. Here the viticulturist asks: Why did foul-smelling grapes appear in place of the proper fruit? The rhetorical ploy here is decidedly different. Neither the farmer nor the members of the assembly know the answer, whereas with the earlier question the answer was clear to all. The difference between the presumed answers to these two questions is highlighted by their quite diverse grammatical structure. The controlling verb in the first is an infinitive construct, a finite verb rules the second. However, the author has linked together all four cola that make up these questions by including the Hebrew verb ʿśh in all four cola: lăʿăśôt in the first, ʿăśîtî in the second, lăʿăśôt in the third, and wayyaʿaś in the fourth. In so doing, the poet has provided for both semantic parallelism and alliterative parallelism, with an emphasis on making and doing, both by the farmer and, surprisingly, by the vineyard in the second question.

After the questions that create a defense for the farmer, he moves to language of judgment or sentence. Again the legal assembly is silent, a silence that apparently enables the farmer to act as sole judge. Nonetheless, the discourse still occurs within the legal assembly, since the second person personal pronoun in v. 5, "you," must refer to those already addressed in v. 3, the first part of the farmer's speech. This sentence is introduced by a disjunctive clause, which itself commences with the introductory word "and now." The bicolon that makes up 5:5a is long 3 + 3 (perhaps even four) accents (9 + 10 syllables). The bicolon does not comprise two balanced clauses but instead expresses one thought: "And now, I will tell you//what I will do to my vineyard." (The ʿśh theme, which was so prominent in v. 4b, continues in v. 5a and provides for semantic parallelism across the boundaries of the primary divisions of this poem.)

The rhythm of the farmer's judgmental language changes decisively in the ensuing cola, vv. 5b-6. Instead of the long, almost prosaic statement in v. 5a, we find a lapidary collocation of destructive language. In v. 5b, the rhythm is clear, two two-accent bicola: "I will remove its hedge and it shall be devoured / I will break down its wall; it shall be trampled down//." The consistency of rhythm is reinforced by parallel syntax and word order: infinitive absolute followed by object with pronominal suffix in the first colon with waw conversive plus hāyāh lĕ and noun, indicating result in the second colon. Although the first person pronoun "I" properly appears in English translation, there is no explicitly first person element in the Hebrew morphology. Instead, the tone is impersonal; one could translate in a woodenly literal way, "there shall be a removal of its hedge." In v. 6, however, the first verb, here a finite verb, "I will make it a waste," does include an explicit first person element. In v. 6a, one finds a tricolon followed by a three-accent bicolon. The tricolon is even more tightly packed than the bicolon that initiated the language of punishment. The lines read (1) I will make it a waste, (2) it will not be pruned, (3) it will not be hoed, (4) briers and thorns shall grow up. Of these cola, only the last has

three accents; the others have only two accents. One is struck here by
the prominence of verbs and, consequently, action: lay waste, prune,
hoe, grow. Although these verses are carefully crafted, they are not
really surprising. Any Israelite farmer could have done such to a garden that did not yield appropriately.

The same cannot be said for the final bicolon of the farmer's speech.
The verse's final bicolon is, again, long, balancing the bicolon with
which the poetry of judgment began. However, what distinguishes this
colon is not the rhythm but the semantics: "the clouds I will command,
to prevent rain from falling upon it."* The word order is a bit unusual,
since the prepositional phrase "concerning the clouds" appears before
the subject of the verb. We take this word order to be a careful attempt
to veil the identity of the farmer as long as possible. Had the verb
appeared first, that identity would have been known at the very beginning of the bicolon. With this bicolon, the poet reveals that the farmer
is a deity, since only a god could control the rains. This revelation
signals the end of the speech of this individual, now known to be
Yahweh.

In vv. 5-6, the poet uses the elements of rhythm and semantics in
a particularly prominent way. He does so with another element, which
we have not yet mentioned: allusion. In lists of treaty or covenant
curses, both biblical and extra-biblical, the notions of unproductive
land (Lev. 26:20; Deut. 28:16) and drought (Deut. 28:22-24) are prominent. Specific mention of weeds, "briers and thorns," v. 5, is probably
also a part of this tradition. Isaiah 34, a text replete with covenant
curses, mentions weeds, "thorns, nettles and thistles," as a part of a
description of cursed land.[19] This particular element in the legal traditions of the ancient Near East, namely, curse language, has been
appropriated in this speech of the divine winemaker. The poet has
adopted the ploy of literary allusion to covenant curse traditions in
order to make the language of legal sentence especially vigorous, since
it is language connected intimately with Israel's understanding of its
relationship with Yahweh.

In Isa. 5:7, the poet returns to the voice of the lover, who had spoken in vv. 1-2. This change is marked by the emphatic particle kî,
"indeed," and by an extraordinarily long line: "Indeed, the vineyard of
Yahweh of Hosts is the house of Israel."* This statement includes no
action verbs, and with good reason. It is designed to provide interpretive information, not to narrate action. Some of the information is not
even new. On the basis of the last bicolon in Isa. 5:6, the listener or

reader knows that Yahweh is the owner of the vineyard. The new information involves the identity of the vineyard, that it is the house of Israel. And with this information, we enter the world of allegory, or something very much like it.[20] In an allegory, every important element may be translated into some reality external to the imagery of the poem. So, according to the beloved as exegete, the vineyard signifies the house of Israel, the men of Judah refers to that which the wine maker planted, and, elliptically, the expected grapes represented justice and righteousness, and the wild grapes, bloodshed and a cry. Such allegorical interpretation makes clear that which might not be understood, even by the attentive audience or reader. Certain human activity, which may be characterized by the nouns "bloodshed" and "cry" required the legal sentence, which has already been fully described. Put another way, the action of the deity as farmer is already clear. The allegory does not interpret vv. 3-6. Instead, the allegorical interpretation jumps back to vv. 1-2. This jump underlines the envelope structure of this poem, namely, the relative independence of vv. 1-2 and 7, which almost may be read as a sensible unit in its own right. The poet could have written the verses in an order like 1-2, 7, 3-6. However, the ambiguity, which we have mentioned earlier, functioned to create interest and intrigue on the part of the hearer. Hence the ambiguity about the identity of the farmer is resolved only at the end of his speech. And the identity of the other parties, expressed allegorically, is revealed only in the final verse of the poem. Everything happens— or put another way, the piling up of verbs occurs—before we are clear about who is perpetrating what. Moreover, there is an ironic touch. We now know that those who had been called to judge (v. 3) are, at the conclusion, condemned. The poem functions to accuse and announce judgment.

As befits such a carefully formulated poem, the final lines are highly refined. Verse 7a,b links language from vv. 1-2, that of vineyard and planting, to the group or groups mentioned in the deity's speech, namely, the individuals of Judah. Moreover, the final line as well returns to the earlier language of the poem, the verb *qwh*, "looked for," which had occurred in v. 2. However, the key element in the line is the wordplay: justice-*mišpāṭ* and bloodshed-*miśpāḥ*; righteousness-*ṣĕdāqāh*, and cry-*ṣĕʿāqāh*. This linking of assonance and alliteration underscores a key issue in the poem, namely, the difference between that which was expected and that which appeared: good grapes versus stinking fruit; the difference between justice and bloodshed and between righteousness and a cry. Put in a slightly more pointed way, the poet has highlighted the difference between that which was expected and that which eventuated by presenting nouns that sound alike. The phonetic similarity underscores the profound difference between, for example, justice and bloodshed. The difference between the good and the bad fruit is expressed here in the semantic difference between nouns that sound alike.

It is important to note that certain ambiguities remain even after one reads through the poem with care. We are still not certain about the identity of the singer, although it is presumably the prophet. The more important element of ambiguity rests on the second question of the farmer: "why did it yield wild grapes?" or to use the language of the allegorical interpretation, "why did it yield bloodshed and a cry?" This question remains unanswered, left for hearer and reader to ponder. Surely one element of this poet's artistry is the ploy of unresolved ambiguity.

In sum, Isa. 5:1-7 is a remarkably complex poem. It presents a song, sung by the deity as viticulturist, which is surrounded by introduction and conclusion, verses uttered by the deity's beloved, presumably the prophet. The poem is made up of a complex, envelope structure utilizing two songs. One of the prominent devices used in this poem is, therefore, that of changing voices.[21] In addition, the creative use of ambiguity early in the poem, the appropriation of legal language (v. 3) and the allusion to curse traditions (vv. 5-6), the presence and absence of verbs (and its corollary, varying pace), and the allegorical style of interpretation (v. 7) provide much of the richness in this brief prophetic poem.

PSALM 1

The book of Psalms presents issues for interpreters unlike those raised either by poems embedded in narrative texts, for example, Deuteronomy 32, or by poetry in the prophetic corpus, even when a complete poem seems discernible, for example, Isa. 5:1-7. First, unlike prophetic poetry, it is usually easy to determine the extent of an individual poetic unit in the Psalter. The beginnings and endings of over three quarters of the psalms are marked by various titles or superscriptions, for example, "A Psalm of David."[22] As a result, there are few questions about the boundaries of the poems.

Second, the process by which the Psalter was compiled presents fewer redaction-critical problems for the interpreter of an individual psalm than does that which lies behind the pentateuchal or prophetic poetry. That is, the surrounding psalms provide little specific information for the interpretation of a given psalm, even though several psalms may belong to an early collection, for example, the Elohistic psalter (Psalms 42–72). Hence the interpreter regularly focuses almost exclusively on an individual psalm, and not the psalm within its literary surroundings.

Third, interpreters typically do not question the view that the psalms are poetry. There is no consensus, however, that the reader must begin reading psalms with poetic eyes and ears. But reading and analyzing the psalms as poetry is central to the interpretive process. An examination of commentaries on the Psalms illustrates the lack of attention given to poetic considerations. While commentary introductions usually have a brief discussion of Hebrew prosody, one rarely finds more than a listing of rhythmic patterns and/or occasional comment on the type of cola used. Those interested in determining the original social settings, for example, the liturgical setting, have suggested that poetic influences may even "interfere" with this enterprise.[23] However, since ancient poetic strategies arose within social settings, it seems misleading to regard poetic and social factors as unrelated. Rather, identifying these diverse influences can enrich the interpretive perspectives.

Fourth, the historical dating of particular psalms is complicated. The general consensus of scholarship is that over two-thirds of them are dated in the postexilic period. Since the extensive form-critical work on the psalms, the tendency has been less to seek historical periods or events behind these texts and more to identify the cultic or other social settings that may be implied. Explicit historical allusions are rare in the psalms. On the other hand, form criticism has given us a rich and complex history of genre analysis on the poems in the Psalter. Although the interpreter often confronts diverse names for the same genre, this variation in terminology does not present an insurmountable interpretive problem. More complicated, however, is the task of integrating the form-critically based identification of genres with the poetic analysis of a psalm. Our task includes analyzing a psalm poetically, in a way that might incorporate earlier form critical work.

Since the Psalter commences with Psalm 1,[24] the interpreter confronts no problems in determining the beginning of this poem. However, since the second psalm in the Psalter does not begin with a superscription, one must raise a question about the end of Psalm 1. The textual history and interpretation of Psalm 1 in Christianity and Judaism yield diverse theories regarding whether or not Psalm 1 might more appropriately be interpreted together with Psalm 2.[25] The inclusio in Pss. 1:1 and 2:11—for example, "happy/bless," "way," "perish" in 1:1 and 2:11—have led some modern interpreters to see the two as a single psalm. Some textual traditions of Acts 13:33 cite v. 7 of the second psalm as though it came from the first psalm in the Psalter.[26] The extensive use of Psalm 2 in the New Testament (it is one of the most frequently cited psalms), where the focus is on messianic themes, seems not to draw on the motifs of Psalm 1, whereas the royal imagery of Psalm 2 is transferred with some ease to various early church understandings of Jesus. We would contend that the poetic analysis, genre issues, dominant motifs, and a series of other arguments sustain the conclusion that Ps. 1:1-6 may be understood as an interpretive unit or poem separable from Ps. 2:1-11.

Although it is impossible to date Psalm 1 precisely, it is usually understood as postexilic, along with other so-called wisdom psalms. The focus on torah ("law") and the strong, sharp distinctions between the "good" and the "bad" support a later date. As one interpreter has said, the first psalm comes from a time when the "responsibility that once was primarily that of Israel's leaders is laid squarely on the shoulders of the pious."[27] This perspective is encountered frequently in postexilic literature. The redaction-critical issue of Psalm 1 centers on its introductory character. Many think it was written for this spot in the Psalter or at least brought there as a prologue.[28] Certainly the "wicked," "sinners," and "scoffers" are exposed fully throughout the Psalter as obstacles to anyone wishing to become happy or blessed. Similarly, a central theme heard throughout the Psalter has to do with those singing about the LORD knowing the way of the righteous. Whether or not Psalm 1 was written for this prestigious spot or was brought here to introduce the collection would not change significantly the postexilic date maintained by historical criticism.

Psalm 1 is most frequently classified as a wisdom or didactic poem. Some scholars understand this designation as a form-critical observation, for example, based on attention to typical structures, formulas, and indications of common earlier oral stages.[29] Others argue that designating a text as a didactic poem is based more on content.[30] Certainly only a few, often those who see Psalms 1 and 2 as a single unit, disagree with the wisdom genre designation. There are variations in the understandings of the settings out of which sapiential genres emerged. These variations surround the question of the relationship of wisdom poetry to the ritual life of Israel. The separation of wicked and righteous, focus on the torah, and concern not to associate with the outsider are issues in Psalm 1. These are both communal and individual concerns within Israel. However, the contention that a communal situation generated wisdom poems, as opposed to thinking of more private, literary origins, remains a complicated issue. A close reading of Psalm 1 will demonstrate how this tightly crafted poem addresses both communal and individual concerns. More important, the highly literate context of Psalm 1 and its association with wisdom literature will become clear.

Poetic analysis of Psalm 1 may begin with consideration of rhythm. The poem's rhythmic patterns are extremely irregular, as is apparent in almost any English translation. Starting with the first words, one is confronted with a line that seems either too short ("Happy/Blessed is the individual"*) or too long, "Happy the one who has not walked in the counsel of the wicked."* Other lines in the psalm, when analyzed through either stress or syllable counting, present a similar dilemma. Since there is no dominant rhythm in the poem, most interpreters focus their interpretation on other poetic features.[31]

The numerous, small linking words—"who," "nor," "but," "and," "therefore," "for"—lead the reader from one line to another. While poetry normally does not link lines or strophes with these particles, their presence requires the reader to discern their functions. First, they require the reader to look carefully at the syntactical links between cola. They underscore the diverse parallelism within the psalm. The opposition of two kinds of individuals, the "wicked" and the "righteous," is boldly contrasted and compared not only through the connectives but also by word pairs, contrasting similes, and other techniques. In short, these particles draw the reader's attention to the intense parallelism of this poem.

Second, these small connectives at the beginning of a colon are often said to be an anacrusis, that is, one or more syllables at the beginning of a line that stand outside the rhythm of that line. However, there are too many such words in Psalm 1 to account for them in this manner. On the other hand, the opening monocolon, "Happy the individual,"* stands outside the psalm's strophic structure. This anacrusis governs the poem in diverse ways.[32] Since this colon is rhythmically separated from the rest of the poem, the reader will recognize the importance of its words, which, after all, are the first ones in the Psalter. They point to the central individual, the blessed individual, who is the focus of this entire collection of poetry.

The initial tricolon then sets out three chiastically structured descriptions,

> who does not walk in the counsel of the wicked,
> and in the way of sinners does not stand,
> or in the gathering of scoffers does not dwell.*

Our translation preserves, as closely as possible, the Hebrew word order. The first colon begins with the negation (*lō'*) plus the verb followed by the prepositional phrase, while the last two cola reverses this order.

negation + verb	prepositional phrase
prepositional phrase	negation + verb

Semantic correspondence is grammatically reinforced through the repetition of the negated verbs, the preposition "in," and the plural objects of the preposition. These three negative qualities in the tricolon contrast with the happy or blessed individual addressed in the anacrusis. Within the Psalter one would normally have expected "counsel" to have been of the LORD or something "good" (Pss. 73:24; 106:13; 119:24), just as "way" often is associated with a positive direction (Ps. 119:1, 3, 14, 37). In contrast to these reversed expectations, a paradigmatic association exists between "wicked," "sinners," and "scoffers." The list of negative qualities ascribed to the blessed person runs from associating ("walk") with disqualified individuals to then standing with them, and finally "dwelling" with them, a description that many commentators have understood as intensifying the relationship. We call this a syntagmatic connection in that these negative qualities build from a loose relationship to one that constitutes "living" with the other. This chiastic tricolon signals within the first verse the poem's dominant literary features: chiasmus and contrast. But it does that with both grammatic and semantic correspondence.

The second verse is a bicolon,

> but in the torah of the LORD is his delight,
> and in his torah he murmurs day and night.*

It stands in contrast to the first tricolon by describing two positive activities of the individual. Our translation makes clear that both lines begin with a prepositional phrase following the small connectives. They repeat the preposition ("in"), which is also found three times in the first tricolon of v. 1. In each of the five lines of the two cola, "in" appears at the beginning of the line immediately following small linking words. One can hear the phonologic repetition that holds together the tricolon and the bicolon despite the semantic contrast between the negative and the positive activities. Careful attention to repetitive elements, even as small as the preposition "in," assists the reader.

There is, in addition, another important element of a phonologic and semantic repetition that supports an understanding of Psalm 1 as a single poetic entity. The negative particle *lō'* is repeated three times in the first tricolon, once in v. 3 at the conclusion of the simile ("their leaves do not wither"), in the crucial hinge of v. 4a ("Not so the wicked"), and in v. 5 ("the wicked will not arise"). To observe the prominence and function of these elements in providing coherence within Psalm 1 enables us to distinguish it from Psalm 2.

Still more poetic elements are at work in Psalm 1. The initial anacrusis ("Happy the individual") includes two repeated consonants, including the first letter of the Hebrew alphabet (aleph). The repeated preposition "in" (*bĕ*) is the second letter of the Hebrew alphabet (beth). It has been observed that the last word of the psalm begins with the last letter of the Hebrew alphabet (taw).[33] This incipient alphabetic acrostic raises the question of the purpose. Why might an acrostic form have been used in Psalm 1? There is little argument that acrostics have visual appeal. Some scholars have thought they also may have phonetic, that is, alliterative, appeal.[34] Since literary devices employing phonologic elements are prominent in Psalm 1, it may be appropriate to reexamine the phonologic features of the acrostic, keeping in mind that an important conceptual force of the acrostic is to signal completeness and comprehensiveness. This psalm embraces all that a happy/blessed individual needs for living life according to the LORD's precepts. An acrostic is suited to this emphasis on totality. The happy individual's murmuring of the torah further enforces the relationship between phonology and conceptual integration as adumbrated by the incipient acrostic.

Paired similes[35] stand at the center of vv. 3 and 4. The first simile compares the happy individual to a tree, which is located where it will flourish. The tree serves as the vehicle. The tenor of the image conveys "stability, durability, freshness, productivity."[36] This figure of speech provides a contrast to the second simile, in which chaff represents the ephemeral, dead, and useless. The contrast between the similes is heightened by the ellipsis in the chaff simile. The single verb ("driven away") appears in the first part of the colon but is understood in the second half as well, that is, a case of gapping, or ellipsis. The tree is the focus of attention, the subject, through at least three lines. There is no gapping, or ellipsis, with the verbs in the tree simile. In fact, the tricolon with the three verbs in the tree simile over against the brevity of the chaff simile and the gapping point to the emphasis on everything that has to do with the happy individual. Finally, the contrast is heightened through similarity. There is a phonetic echoing in the similes. Not only is the comparative ("like") repeated but the poem echoes with the phonetic similarity of the words for tree and chaff, that is, both are monosyllabic words ending with the same Hebrew consonant ($ṣ$). The reader hears phonologic similarity within the context of remarkable semantic contrast.

All that remains within vv. 3 and 4 are the lines

> and in all that he does he prospers—
> Not so the wicked!*

The first part of Psalm 1 is drawn to a conclusion by the last line of v. 3. The Hebrew grammar permits one to read the subject of the prospering as either tree—thus a continuation of the simile—or the happy individual. In our judgment, the poet created intentional ambiguity, since the tree clearly is prospering, and by analogy so also will the happy individual, the one who focuses on the torah. The simile extends and elaborates on the nature of the happy individual. "Not so the wicked" shouts the antithesis to everything from the beginning of v. 1b ("who does not walk in the counsel of the wicked"*) to the end of v. 3. The tricolon in v. 1 began with the wicked, and the bicolon discussed here sets up the contrast with the repetition of the wicked. The poem presents the reader with a hinge on which the poem turns—from the one who prospers to the one who does not prosper.

This hinge provides a significant clue for the identification of a chiastic structure that undergirds the entire poem, except for the initial anacrusis and concluding bicolon.

A Description of the righteous (vv. 1b-2)
   B Simile (v. 3a-b)
      C Objectifying conclusion (v. 3c)
      C' Objectifying introduction (v. 4a)
   B' Simile (v. 4b)
A' Description of the wicked (v. 5)

The hinge links the more elaborate discussion of the righteous person with the very brief description of the wicked one. There are twice as many words regarding the righteous as there are about the wicked. The poem is not about the wicked, nor is it an elaboration on the two ways. Rather, it uses the negative way to illumine the way of the happy individual.

There are numerous syntactic and semantic similarities between the two parts of the chiasm.[37] The small linking words continue into the second part. Several of them are even identical with those found earlier in the poem. There is no better place to examine the correspondences within the chiasm than by comparing the bicolon in v. 5 with the tricolon in v. 1. The verbs in both cola are negated; the preposition *be*, "in," appears three times in v. 1 and is repeated twice in v. 5; and the words "wicked" and "sinners" are used in both verses. The most intriguing poetic device signaling the correspondence between these two elements in the chiasm is structured in the phonological play between "counsel (*'ăsat*) of the wicked" and "assembly (*'ădat*) of the righteous." Embedded in this correspondence is the recognition of an enormous semantic contrast between the valued "assembly of the righteous" and the despised "counsel of the wicked."

The correspondences within the larger chiastic structure point to both comparison and contrast. For example, the ellipsis or verb gapping, which occurs in v. 5, was not used in v. 1 for the description of the happy individual. Three verbs exist in v. 1, one in each colon. Whereas in v. 5 the verb "will not arise" stands in the first half of the bicolon, there is no verb in the second half. One may discern verb gapping only in v. 2, and there the verb appears in the second half of the bicolon, not in the first half as in v. 5. Furthermore, the tree simile includes three verbs with no gapping, just as the tricolon of v. 1. The chaff simile uses only one verb, which points to the insubstantial character of that described in the simile in comparison to that conveyed by the tree simile.

The chiastic structure and the elements of contrast so central to this poem receive a final emphasis in the concluding bicolon of v. 6. The description of the righteous (vv. 1-2) began by speaking of the wicked. The section on the wicked (vv. 4-5) ends by speaking of the righteous. The conclusion reverses that order,

> For the LORD watches over the way of the righteous,
> but the way of the wicked will perish.

For the first time in the poem, the LORD becomes the subject. The verb "watches over," or as often translated "knows," implies a "special intimacy."[38] In the midst of numerous words used repeatedly in the psalm, a new actor has appeared. However, this "theophany" comes as no surprise, since the LORD's torah or instruction was so central to the description of the happy individual (v. 2). There is no exact equivalence stated between the group identified as the righteous, who are known by Yahweh, and the happy individual, except for the association that the poem urges the reader to make between the delight of the happy individual and the group known by the LORD.

The poem does not end with the first half of the bicolon; it continues to delineate briefly the fate of the wicked. One is therefore enticed to read on in the book of Psalms to discover how the righteous and the wicked stand in contrast and what their respective fates will be. In this first psalm the reader discovers that they are described through characterizations that are both semantically and grammatically contrasted. However, the opposition between the "wicked" and the "righteous" is also phonologically and grammatically held together as though each one needs the other in order for their respective destinies to be comprehensible.

97

Notes

CHAPTER 1: Understanding Hebrew Poetry

1. Robert Alter and Frank Kermode, *The Literary Guide to the Bible* (Cambridge: Harvard University Press, 1987), 611–24.

2. That poetry demands special attention is also attested now in several volumes on Psalms that were designed for the general reader, e.g., a chapter entitled "Poetry and Interpretation," in Patrick D. Miller, Jr., *Interpreting the Psalms* (Philadelphia: Fortress Press, 1986), and "The Journey to the Psalmist's Language," in Mark S. Smith, *Psalms: The Divine Journey* (New York: Paulist Press, 1987).

3. So, for example, the article "Characteristics of Hebrew Poetry," *The New Oxford Annotated Bible*, 1523–29, and Norman K. Gottwald, "Poetry, Hebrew," *The Interpreter's Dictionary of the Bible* (Nashville: Abingdon Press, 1962), 3:829-38.

4. For an excellent discussion of the term *selāh*, see Peter C. Craigie, *Psalms 1–50*, WBC 19 (Waco, Tex.: Word Books, 1983), 76–77.

5. The third quatrain of Gray's "Elegy Written in a Country Churchyard" in its earliest and latest forms reads:

Save that from yonder ivy-mantled tow'r
The moping owl does to the moon complain
Of such as, wand'ring near her secret bow'r
Molest her ancient solitary reign.

Being in the dimly lit church graveyard could lead one to have voiced "sacred bower," but the poetic, antique ambiguities of bower are better reinforced by the adjective "secret" which adds mystery to the already "sacred."

6. For the classic exposition, see Robert Lowth, *Lectures on the Sacred Poetry of the Hebrews*, trans. G. Gregory (London: S. Chadwick & Co., 1847) originally published as *De Sacra poesi Hebraeorum* (Oxford: Clarendon, 1753).

7. R. O. Evans, "Parallelism," *The Princeton Handbook of Poetic Terms*, ed. Alex Preminger et al., (Princeton: Princeton University Press, 1986), 183. (Hereafter cited as *PHPT*.)

8. Stanley Fish, *Is There a Text in This Class? The Authority of Interpretive Communities* (Cambridge: Harvard University Press, 1982), 322–37.

9. Plato, *Phaedrus* 245a, 265.

10. J. G. von Herder, *The Spirit of Hebrew Poetry* (Burlington, Vt.: Edward Smith, 1833), 2:10.

11. James Muilenburg, "Isaiah, Introduction, Chs. 40–66," *The Interpreter's Bible* (New York: Abingdon Press, 1956), 5:382.

12. The literary-critical work of Phyllis Trible may be cited in this regard, *God and the Rhetoric of Sexuality* (Philadelphia: Fortress Press, 1978), 8–12.

13. "Preface to Lyrical Ballads," in *English Literature and Its Backgrounds*, vol. 2: *From the Forerunners of Romanticism to the Present*, ed. Bernard D. Grebanier et al., rev. ed. (New York: Dryden Press, 1949), 336.

14. *Peacock's Four Ages of Poetry, Shelley's Defense of Poetry, Browning's Essay on Shelley*, ed. H. F. B. Brett-Smith, Folcroft Library Editions (Oxford: Basil Blackwell, 1977), 17.

15. Ibid., 48–55.

16. Robert Alter, *The Art of Biblical Poetry* (New York: Basic Books, 1985), 87.

17. Michael O'Connor, *Hebrew Verse Structure* (Winona Lake, Ind.: Eisenbrauns, 1980); and Stephen A. Geller, "Theory and Method in the Study of Hebrew Poetry," *JQR* 73 (1982): 77.

18. James L. Kugel, *The Idea of Biblical Poetry: Parallelism and Its History* (New Haven: Yale University Press, 1981); and Francis Landy, "Poetics and Parallelism: Some comments on James Kugel's 'The Idea of Biblical Poetry,'" *JSOT* 28 (1984): 74–81.

19. Adele Berlin, *The Dynamics of Biblical Parallelism* (Bloomington, Ind.: Indiana University Press, 1985), 17.

20. Ibid., 135.

21. M. H. Abrams, "Theories of Poetry," *PHPT*, 208–12.

22. Such as Jacques Derrida, *Writings and Difference*, trans. Alan Bass (Chicago: University of Chicago Press, 1978).

23. Susan A. Handelman, *The Slayers of Moses: The Emergence of Rabbinic Interpretation in Modern Literary Theory* (Albany, N.Y.: State University of New York Press, 1982), 222.

24. Handelman's *The Slayers of Moses* is one of the most illuminating discussions of how various dimensions of rabbinic interpretation have influenced contemporary figures such as Harold Bloom, Jacques Derrida, and Jacques Lacan.

25. Abrams, "Theories of Poetry," *PHPT*, 213.

26. Alter, *The Art of Biblical Narrative*, 50.

27. Geller, "Theory and Method," 66, 75–77. Cf. James L. Kugel, "Some Thoughts on Future Research Into Biblical Style: Addenda to *The Idea of Biblical Poetry*," *JSOT* 28 (1984): 110–12.

28. Indicative of much recent work on Hebrew poetry, as represented by papers presented at the Society of Biblical Literature's annual meetings, is the volume edited by Elaine R. Follis, *Directions in Biblical Hebrew Poetry*,

JSOTSS 40 (Sheffield, Eng.: JSOT Press, 1987). Most of the papers included in the volume could be construed either as concern for the Bible as literature, e.g., attention to particular literary techniques, or as concern for the interpretation of texts. Only Freedman's paper addresses the technical issues of prosody.

29. The classic exposition of the views of Frank Moore Cross and David Noel Freedman is presented in their jointly authored Ph.D. dissertation, *Studies in Ancient Yahwistic Poetry* (Johns Hopkins University, 1950), now available as SBLDS 21 (Missoula, Mont.: Scholars Press, 1975).

30. Julius Ley wrote three influential studies: *Die metrischen Formen der hebräischen Poesie* (Leipzig: B. G. Teubner, 1866); *Grundzüge des Rhythmus des Vers- und Strophenbaues in der hebräischen Poesie: Nebst Analyse einer Auswahl von Psalmen und anderen strophischen Dichtungen der verschiedenen Vers- und Strophenarten mit vorangehendem Abriss der Metrik der hebräischen Poesie* (Halle: Verlag der Buchhandlung des Waisenhauses, 1875); and *Leitfaden der Metrik der hebräischen Poesie nebst dem ersten Buche der Psalmen nach rhythmischer Vers- und Strophenabteilung mit metrischer Analyse* (Halle: Verlag der Buchhandlung des Waisenhauses, 1887). These works influenced not only Eduard Sievers, *Metrische Studien*, vol. 1: *Studien zur hebräischen Metrik* (Leipzig: B. G. Teubner, 1901), but many others, including Albright and his students.

31. Nevertheless we need more comparative work based on other ancient Near Eastern languages, especially Akkadian. So Kugel, "Some Thoughts on Future Research Into Biblical Style," 111–12; cf. Wilfred G. E. Watson, *Classical Hebrew Poetry: A Guide to Its Techniques*, JSOTSS 26 (Sheffield, Eng.: JSOT Press, 1986), 4–5.

32. So A. Cooper, "Two Recent Works on the Structure of Biblical Hebrew Poetry," *JAOS* 110 (1990): 687–90.

33. See the other volumes in this series for examples both of lower criticism, e.g., P. Kyle McCarter, *Textual Criticism: Recovering the Text of the Hebrew Bible*, GBS.OTS (Philadelphia: Fortress Press, 1986), and of higher criticism, e.g., Gene M. Tucker, *Form Criticism of the Old Testament*, GBS.OTS (Philadelphia: Fortress Press, 1971).

34. Dennis Pardee, *Ugaritic and Hebrew Poetic Parallelism: A Trial Cut ('nt I and Proverbs 2)*, VTSup 39 (Leiden: E. J. Brill, 1988), represents a step in this direction.

35. Frank Moore Cross, Jr., *Canaanite Myth and Hebrew Epic: Essays in the History of the Religion of Israel* (Cambridge: Harvard University Press, 1973).

36. Ibid., 187.

37. Another scholar who often works from perspectives similar to Cross has not deleted *mal'āk* in his reconstruction and translation of the text; so Robert G. Boling, *Judges*, AB 6A (Garden City, N.Y.: Doubleday & Co., 1975), 114.

38. Alter, *The Art of Biblical Poetry*, 146.

39. Ibid., 154.

40. See the standard commentaries, e.g., Hans Wildberger, *Jesaja 13–27*, BKAT X/2 (Neukirchen-Vluyn: Neukirchener Verlag, 1978), 892–911; and

more focused studies, such as William R. Millar, *Isaiah 24–27 and the Origin of Apocalyptic*, HSM 11 (Missoula, Mont.: Scholars Press, 1976).

CHAPTER 2: Parallelism

1. Robert Lowth, *Lectures on the Sacred Poetry of the Hebrews*, trans. G. Gregory (London: S. Chadwick & Co., 1847), 210.

2. Ibid., 219.

3. Ibid., lectures 18–34.

4. "Poetry," *HBD*, 804–6, and sections of *HBC*, 402–6, are two exceptions, since they were written by Kugel. The *New Jerome Biblical Commetary* includes an article written by Aloysius Fitzgerald that does not employ the Lowthian language. In fact, it "avoids" the term "parallelism" "because it is too frequently employed in the restricted sense of semantic balance" (p. 204).

5. Especially in George B. Gray, *The Forms of Hebrew Poetry*, with Prolegomenon by D. N. Freedman (New York: KTAV, 1972).

6. Gottwald, *IDB*, 3:830.

7. P. Van der Lugt, *Strofische structuren in de bibels-hebreeuwse poëzie* (Kampen: Kok, 1980).

8. For a further discussion of "line," one could turn to either the *PHPT* or Barbara Herrnstein-Smith, *Poetic Closure: A Study of How Poems End* (Chicago: University of Chicago Press, 1968).

9. Stephen A. Geller, *Parallelism in Early Biblical Poetry*, HSM 20 (Missoula, Mont.: Scholars Press, 1979), 14.

10. Watson, *Classical Hebrew Poetry*, 185–90.

11. Lowth, *Lectures*, 216.

12. Ibid., 210.

13. Ibid., 215.

14. It is difficult to ascertain from the editors and translators of Lowth's work whether this was actually his translation. It is the one that appears in the English text of Lowth.

15. Lowth, *Lectures*, 216.

16. Gray, *Forms of Hebrew Poetry*, esp. 50.

17. By far the most thorough, authoritative, and recent discussion is in Geller, *Parallelism*, Appendix B, 375–85.

18. Gottwald, *IDB*, 3:832.

19. Berlin uses the word "aspect" in part to avoid speaking of types or categories of parallelism. We think this is a useful term to employ.

20. Kugel, *The Idea of Biblical Poetry*, 64.

21. Geller (*Parallelism*, 35) understands lists as one of the simple categories of semantic parallelism closely related to synonymous parallelism. On the other hand, Watson (*Classical Hebrew Poetry*, 351) seems to understand lists, not directly in terms of parallelism, but as a secondary poetic technique.

22. Geller, *Parallelism*, 30.

23. Kugel contended in his original book that "there is no word for 'poetry' in biblical Hebrew. . . . Thus, to speak of 'poetry' at all in the Bible will be in some measure to impose a concept foreign to the biblical world" (*The

Idea of Biblical Poetry, 69). In a later work, he has stated that he had not intended to abandon the distinction between poetry and prose ("Some Thoughts on Future Research Into Biblical Style," 107–17).

24. The current discussions within Hebrew poetry often refer to Roman Jakobson's formulation of a poetic function found in all literature, namely, that "the poetic function projects the principle of equivalence from the axis of selection into the axis of combination" ("Closing Statement: Linguistics and Poetics," in *Style in Language,* ed. Thomas A. Sebeok [Cambridge, Mass.: Technology Press of MIT, 1960], 358). See Berlin, *Dynamics,* 7–17, and Landy, "Poetics and Parallelism," 68–72, for a fuller discussion of these issues.

25. There are two issues, among others, that are involved in the decisions about the printing of poetic and prose texts. First, and directly related to our discussion, is the decision about whether a text is poetry or prose. English and Hebrew readers could look at the various translations of Genesis 9 to see how editors of both Hebrew and English texts have made varying decisions about what portions of the chapter are poetry. Second, even when it is agreed that the text is poetic there are varying decisions about lineation or the distinguishing of cola (cf. pp. 4–5 above). In addition to the texts cited in the introduction, Exodus 15 exemplifies the varied understanding of lineation and hence types of parallelism observed in the same text by different translators and scholars. From fifty to seventy cola have been identified in Exodus 15.

26. Miller, *Interpreting the Psalms,* 30.

27. Berlin, *Dynamics,* 18.

28. Ibid., 64. Berlin uses lexical in combination with semantic categories to refer to parallelism at the level of the word (*lexis*). Psalm 111:6 illustrates lexical parallelism. "The power of his deeds he told to his *people*/ On giving to them the inheritance of *nations*" (Berlin's translation, *Dynamics,* 81). The first colon is not syntactically parallel with the second colon, nor are people and nations semantically parallel. However, the two words are parallel at the lexical level, or as might be said, they are word pairs.

29. This volume is not the place to develop an extended discussion on the differing definitions of such terms as grammar, linguistics, poetics, semantics, and syntax. One could consult an unabridged dictionary, where these terms are discussed, or turn to *PHPT.*

30. *PHPT,* 115.

31. Major works that have specifically developed grammatic parallelism or used it in significant ways: Berlin; Geller; O'Connor; Pardee; Terence Collins, *Line-Forms in Hebrew Poetry: A Grammatical Approach to the Stylistic Study of the Hebrew Prophets,* Studia Pohl, Series Maior, 17 (Rome: Pontifical Biblical Institute, 1978); E. Greenstein, "How Does Parallelism Mean?" in *A Sense of Text,* Jewish Quarterly Review Supplement (Winona Lake, Ind.: Eisenbrauns, 1982), 41–70; Paul E. Dion, *Hebrew Poetics: A Student's Guide* (Mississauga, Ont., Canada: Benben Publications, 1988); and Paul R. Raabe, *Psalm Structures: A Study of Psalms with Refrains,* JSOTSS 104 (Sheffield, Eng.: Sheffield Academic Press, 1990).

32. Pardee, *Ugaritic and Hebrew Poetic Parallelism,* 170. We will not say much about repetitive parallelism, since when working with translations

one can often not be certain about the degree to which translators have indeed repeated identical terms in the translational language. Repetitive parallelism, however, remains an extremely important dimension of Hebrew poetry.

33. Berlin, *Dynamics*, 72–80 and 90–91.

34. Watson, *Classical Hebrew Poetry*, has a separate chapter on "Sound in Hebrew Poetry," 223–50, understanding it as one of the "poetic devices."

35. Collins's entire classification system is based on "line-types" which are identified by syntactical word order.

36. Berlin, *Dynamics*, 104.

37. Watson, *Classical Hebrew Poetry*, 227.

38. Greenstein, "How Does Parallelism Mean?" 41–70.

39. Watson, *Classical Hebrew Poetry*, 118. Part of the futility in trying to delineate categories can be seen in Watson's more recent effort at listing categories in a review of Kugel's work (*JSOT* 28 [1984], 89–98). Here he ends up with five major headings (structural, grammatical, syntactic, semantic, and other), but twenty-four subdivisions!

40. Watson, *Classical Hebrew Poetry*, chap. 6.

41. The now oft quoted Kugel formulation of parallelism (Kugel, *The Idea of Biblical Poetry*, 8).

42. David J. A. Clines, "The Parallelism of Greater Precision," in Follis, *Directions in Biblical Hebrew Poetry*, 95.

CHAPTER 3: Meter and Rhythm

1. So, most recently, Pardee. *Ugaritic and Hebrew Poetic Parallelism*, 195.

2. T. Brogan, "Rhythm," *PHPT*, 238.

3. P. Fry, "Meter," *PHPT*, 141.

4. The matter is not quite so simple, however. Some maintain that "meters provide structure whereas rhythms provide movement within that structure" (Brogan, "Rhythm," *PHPT*, 239). Cf. the discussion of meter and rhythm in Viktor M. Zirmunskij, *Introduction to Metrics: The Theory of Verse*, Slavistic Printings and Reprintings, vol. 58 (The Hague: Mouton & Co., 1966), 18–23.

5. T. Brogan, "Prosody," *PHPT*, 218–19. Brogan comments further on prosody in a way useful to reflection on Hebrew poetry: "Prosodic structures differ from language to language, for languages differ in their selection and combination among universally available phonetic elements; these are always somehow related, but the nature of their relation varies, so that the characteristics of verse do not always remain the same even in a single language throughout its history, and more than one system of versification, and various interpenetrations of verse and prose, can exist in a language at the same time" (p. 219).

6. Fry, "Meter," *PHPT*, 141.

7. Cited by Kugel, *The Idea of Biblical Poetry*, 141.

8. See the useful review in William Henry Cobb, *A Criticism of Systems of Hebrew Metre: An Elementary Treatise* (Oxford: Clarendon Press, 1905).

9. Accent is very important in biblical Hebrew. Unlike some other Semitic languages, accent in Hebrew may be morphophonemic, which is to say that the very presence of accent on one or another syllable in a word can change the meaning of that word. Sabatino Moscati, ed., *An Introduction to the Comparative Grammar of the Semitic Languages: Phonology and Morphology*, Porta Linguarum Orientalium 6 (Wiesbaden: Otto Harrassowitz, 1964), 67, cites a classic case: *šā́bû*, "they returned," vs. *šābû́*, "they took prisoner." The only difference between these two words is accent, which occurs on the first and second syllables respectively.

10. Cf., however, the claims of Freedman: "In our opinion, the relative importance of stressed syllables in contrast with unstressed syllables has been exaggerated; a count of all the syllables provides a better clue to the metrical patterns of the poems of the Hebrew Bible" (Gray, *The Forms of Hebrew Poetry*, xxxv). Freedman here apparently challenges the position of Sievers, who maintained that the relationship between stressed and unstressed syllables was very important in determining meter.

11. Hans Wildberger, *Jesaja 28–39*, BKAT X/3 (Neukirchen-Vluyn: Neukirchener Verlag, 1982), 1689–91.

12. Such disagreement over the details of scansion does not, however, disprove, in and of itself, the existence of rhythmic patterning or even of meter; so Cleanth Brooks and Robert Penn Warren, *Understanding Poetry*, 3d ed. (New York: Holt, Rinehart & Winston, 1960), 165.

13. It must be said that Wildberger (*Jesaja 28–39*, 1690) does maintain that each change in "meter" is consistent with a change in the content of the poem.

14. See, e.g., the use of these terms in Douglas Stuart, *Studies in Early Hebrew Meter*, HSM 13 (Missoula, Mont.: Scholars Press, 1976), 14–15.

15. Seymour Chatman, *A Theory of Meter*, Janua Linguarum, Series Minor, 36 (The Hague: Mouton & Co., 1965), 18.

16. Ibid., 29.

17. Kugel, *The Idea of Biblical Poetry*, 141.

18. O'Connor, *Hebrew Verse Structure*, 138.

19. "On the basis of our study so far, it is not unreasonable to put forward the hypothesis that in Hebrew poetry the permanent frame of reference is provided by the grammatical structure and the order of constituents. In other words, the line-types and line-forms can be looked on as a system of measurement, determining what is a well formed verse-line and thus performing the same function as the more familiar systems of metre" (Collins, *Line-Forms in Hebrew Poetry*, 251).

20. Alter, *The Art of Biblical Poetry*, 9.

21. Dennis Pardee, "Ugaritic and Hebrew Metrics," in *Ugarit in Retrospect: Fifty Years of Ugarit and Ugaritic*, ed. Gordon D. Young (Winona Lake, Ind.: Eisenbrauns, 1981), 115.

22. Gottwald, *IDB*, 3:834.

23. Alter, *The Art of Biblical Poetry*, 19.

24. Johann Döller, *Rhythmus, Metrik und Strophik in der biblisch-hebräischen Poesie* (Paderborn: Ferdinand Schöningh, 1899), 97.

25. To the best of our knowledge, the term "rhythmic pattern" has not

been used to describe the phenomenon to which we are attributing the phrase. Collins (*Line-Forms in Hebrew Poetry*, 272–73) does use the phrase, though apparently not in a technical sense. The pattern important for him is the grammatical one, the "line-form," which, although it obviously entails the inherent rhythm of human language, is not in the first instance a unit based on an analysis of the rhythm in a particular poem.

26. Brogan, "Rhythm," *PHPT*, 238.

27. Ibid.

28. On "end-stopping," see conveniently, Watson, *Classical Hebrew Poetry*, 332–33.

29. On this, see both Collins, *Line-Forms in Hebrew Poetry*, and O'Connor, *Hebrew Verse Structure*.

30. Brogan, "Rhythm," *PHPT*, 239.

31. One views v. 4 properly as a twofold repetition of the 3 + 2 rhythmic pattern.

CHAPTER 4: Poetic Style

1. Watson, for example, treats these issues under the general rubric of imagery and poetic devices. Alter, by contrast, speaks of, among other things, structures of intensification. Readers familiar with works on Hebrew poetry will know that there are issues and terms to which we have not alluded, such as enjambment and merismus.

2. We do not equate the study of style with stylistics, as that latter term has gained currency in certain literary-critical circles. For a brief discussion of stylistics, see Watson, *Classical Hebrew Poetry*, 3.

3. William F. Thrall and Addison Hibbard, *A Handbook to Literature* (New York: Odyssey Press, 1960), 281–82.

4. Despite this judgment, Fisch seems to suggest that the boundary between simile and metaphor is somewhat permeable; so his discussion of the way metaphors and similes work in the Song of Solomon, Harold Fisch, *Poetry with a Purpose: Biblical Poetics and Interpretation*, ISBL (Bloomington, Ind.: Indiana University Press, 1988), 91–92. Using quite a different approach, Berlin, following Jakobson, finds it possible to construe parallelism as metaphor. In her discussion, Berlin quotes Jakobson to the effect that "'anything sequent is a simile' and 'metonymy is slightly metaphorical and any metaphor has a metonymical tint'" (*Dynamics*, 100). The approaches of Fisch and Berlin demonstrate that one may think in diverse ways about the meaning and function of similes and metaphors.

5. Berlin, *Dynamics*, 101. This judgment is possible because she is willing to discern a simile even when a particle marking comparison is not present; so her discussion of Ps. 125:2 as a simile without the explicit marker and Eccl. 7:1 as a metaphor.

6. See Watson, *Classical Hebrew Poetry*, 257–58.

7. It is interesting to note that metaphors, although they do occur in Hosea's poetry, (e.g., Hos. 4:7; 8:7-8, 9; 10:1, 11-13), are markedly less frequent than are similes. For a recent and valuable discussion of metaphoric

NOTES

language in another prophetic book, see Kirsten Nielsen, *There Is Hope for a Tree: The Tree as Metaphor in Isaiah*, JSOTSS 65 (Sheffield, Eng.: JSOT Press, 1989). Cf. three earlier and more general studies: D. Payne, "A Perspective on the Use of Simile in the Old Testament," *Semitics* 1 (1970): 111–25; D. Rosner, "The Simile and Its Use in the Old Testament," *Semitics* 4 (1974): 37–46; and Claus Westermann, *Vergleiche und Gleichnisse im Alten und Neuen Testament*, CTM 14 (Stuttgart: Calwer Verlag, 1984), esp. 28–31 on Hosea.

8. Cf. C. J. Labuschagne, "The Similes in the Book of Hosea," *Die Ou Testamentiese Werkgemeenskap in Suid-Afrika* 7–8 (Potchefstroom: Pro Rege, 1964–65), 64–76, which is basically an inventory of the various vehicles.

9. Westermann (*Vergleiche*, 31) describes them as deriving from the language of people's lives.

10. See similarly H. W. Wolff, *Hosea: A Commentary on the Book of the Prophet Hosea*, Hermeneia (Philadelphia: Fortress Press, 1974): "The most provocative are his [Hosea's] similes for Yahweh and Israel" (p. xxiv). Westermann (*Vergleiche*, 28) speaks about the limited form-critical contexts in which the similes appear: twenty in the accusation, eighteen in the pronouncement of judgment, whereas they occur only four times in oracles of salvation (Hos. 1:10; 6:1-3; 11:10-11; 14:5-7, 8. In addition, Westermann observes that references to Israel's early history are particularly prominent in Hosea's similes. Westermann argues that Hosea used similes to intensify his rhetoric.

11. The comparison between Yahweh and lions extends into v. 14b, as is suggested by the presence of the verb "rend," which elsewhere (e.g., Ps. 17:12) describes the action of a lion.

12. Many commentators emend the text to insert the appropriate particle. The problem is complex, since the Septuagint provides quite a different reading.

13. Wolff, *Hosea*, 233.

14. The Hebrew is ambiguous. One could also translate: "they will again dwell . . ." In addition, the next colon presents problems, since MT reads "his shadow," whereas many commentators conjecture "my shadow." We follow MT.

15. O'Connor, *Hebrew Verse Structure*, 527–33.

16. Raabe, *Psalm Structures*, a recent monograph on psalms with refrains, presents the best summary of the discussion. It is generally acknowledged that the stanza is not employed in all poetry (cf. *PHPT*, 267–68).

17. Watson, *Classical Hebrew Poetry*, 163.

18. Kugel notes that even in a poem that employs a refrain (Ps. 107: 8, 15, 21, 31), the refrain does not occur at regular intervals (Kugel, *The Idea of Biblical Poetry*, 72 n 19).

19. *PHPT*, 296. Gray used the term, "verse paragraph" to refer to unequal blocks of text that seemingly the reader divided lines into in order to make some sense (Gray, *Forms of Hebrew Poetry*, 192).

20. Watson, *Classical Hebrew Poetry*, 164; D. W. Cotter, *A Study of Job 4–5 in the Light of Contemporary Literary Theology* (Rome: Pontificia Universitas Gregoriana, 1989), 154; and Raabe, *Psalm Structures*, 168ff.

21. Most recently Pardee (*Ugaritic and Hebrew Poetic Parallelism*, 3,

70) has used the term "sense unit," but without much discussion. It is a term that has been employed in exegetical method, not just applied to poetry, by a number of scholars.

CHAPTER 5: Poetic Analysis

1. There have been a number of important studies of Deuteronomy 32: P. Skehan, "The Structure of the Song of Moses in Deuteronomy (Deut. 32:1-43)," *CBQ* 13 (1951): 153–63; Otto Eissfeldt, *Das Lied Moses Deuteronomium 32:1-43 und das Lehrgedicht Asaphs Psalm 78 samt einer Analyse der Umgebung des Mose-Liedes*, Berichte über die Verhandlungen der Sächsischen Akademie der Wissenschaften zu Leipzig; Philologisch-historische Klasse, vol. 104, no. 5 (Berlin: Akademie-Verlag, 1958); W. F. Albright, "Some Remarks on the Song of Moses in Deuteronomy XXXII," *VT* 9 (1959): 339–46; and G. E. Wright, "The Lawsuit of God: A Form-Critical Study of Deuteronomy 32," in *Israel's Prophetic Heritage: Essays in Honor of James Muilenburg*, ed. Bernhard W. Anderson and Walter Harrelson (New York: Harper & Row, 1962), 26–67. In these earlier studies, issues of rhythm, parallelism, and literary techniques receive short shrift. This situation changed, for at least part of the poem, with the appearance of an article by Stephen A. Geller, "The Dynamics of Parallel Verse: A Poetic Analysis of Deut. 32:6-12," *HTR* 75 (1982): 35–56. In this study, Geller focused on "the relationship between form and meaning in parallel verse" as a part of a larger enterprise, namely, to understand and appreciate not only the entire Hebrew poetic system but, on a smaller scale, the individual poem. To this extent, Geller dealt not only with parallelism, which he understood in a way not dissimilar from Adele Berlin, but also with imagery, rhyme, and the like. Geller's work sets the stage for the sort of work we conduct here. With the exception of vv. 10-12, our analysis covers different parts of the poem than does Geller's analysis. A most recent treatment is that of Fisch, "The Song of Moses Pastoral in Reverse," in his *Poetry with a Purpose*, 55–79. He is more interested in "the intertextual weave" that links Deuteronomy 32 with Isaiah 1 and other biblical texts than in a close interpretive reading of the Song of Moses alone.

2. Albright, "Some Remarks on the Song of Moses."

3. Wright, "The Lawsuit of God," 67.

4. See, e.g., S. R. Driver, *A Critical and Exegetical Commentary on Deuteronomy*, ICC (Edinburgh: T. & T. Clark, 1901), 345–47, for arguments for a late preexilic date, and A. D. H. Mayes, *Deuteronomy*, NCBC (Grand Rapids: Wm. B. Eerdmans, 1979), 381–82, as well as A. Phillips, *Deuteronomy*, CBCNEB (Cambridge: Cambridge University Press, 1973), 218–19, for an exilic or postexilic date.

5. H. B. Huffmon, "The Covenant Lawsuit in the Prophets," *JBL* 78 (1959): 285.

6. Wright, "The Lawsuit of God," 43.

7. Cf. Geller's valuable discussion of these verses in his "The Dynamics of Parallel Verse." Geller, in our judgment, correctly notes the bold language and imagery of vv. 10-12: "One is swept up by the dramatic power of a boldly

progressing form, the chain-like structure that links the couplets, and the image of the *nešer*" (p. 55).

8. Were the goal of the journey clearly the divine abode, we would agree with Geller that the author is alluding to "the motif of the eagle bearing the hero into the heavens"; so the Etana myth, Geller, "The Dynamics of Parallel Verse," 53–54.

9. W. Dever, "Asherah, Consort of Yahweh? New Evidence from Kuntillet 'Ajrud," *BASOR* 255 (1984), 21–37.

10. The phrase "heights of the land" occurs in two other places in the Hebrew Bible, Isa. 58:14 and Micah 1:3. On the basis of these occurrences, the phrase appears to signify mountain heights, without the connotation of a cultic high place. Alternatively, one might translate "he enabled him to ride on the back of Earth," a mythological allusion.

11. Cf. Otto Kaiser, *Isaiah 1–12: A Commentary*, OTL (Philadelphia: Westminster Press, 1983), 90: "The so-called 'Song of the Vineyard' is one of the poetic masterpieces of the Old Testament." One may discern some attention to the literary features of this poem in three articles: H. Junker, "Die literarische Art von Is 5:1-7," *Bib* 40 (1959), 259–66; D. Lys, "La vigne et le double je: Exercise de style sur Esaie 5:1-7," VTSup 26, 1–17; and W. Schottroff, "Das Weinberglied Jesajas (Is. 5:1-7): Ein Beitrag zur Geschichte der Parabel," ZAW 82 (1970), 68-91. The most recent comprehensive treatment is that of A. Bjørndalen; *Untersuchungen zur allegorischen Rede der Propheten Amos und Jesaja*, BZAW 165 (Berlin: Walter de Gruyter, 1986), 245–343.

12. J. Vermeylen (*Du prophète Isaïe à l'apocalyptique* [Paris: J. Gabalda, 1977], 1:159–68) has argued that the vocabulary of Isa. 5:1-7 bears strongest resemblances to late monarchic and exilic texts. Further, he maintains that the genre of the text, a lawsuit, depends on the Deuteronomic notions of covenant and that Isa. 5:1-7 may be attributed to the Deuteronomistic circle. Hence, Isa. 5:1-7 must postdate the work of the earliest Deuteronomic formulations, which themselves postdate Isaiah ben Amoz. Finally, he maintains that a survey of texts that he deems to be "parallels" (esp. 2 Sam. 12:1-12 and 1 Kings 20:35-43) suggests an exilic provenance for the poem. Kaiser (*Isaiah 1–2: A Commentary*, 93) defends Vermeylen's assessment.

13. Hermann Barth, *Die Jesaja-Worte in der Josiazeit: Israel und Assur als Thema einer produktiven Neuinterpretation der Jesajaüberlieferung*, WMANT 48 (Neukirchen-Vluyn: Neukirchener Verlag, 1977).

14. Cf. the cogent conjecture for a date "between 733 and 722," R. E. Clements, *Isaiah 1–39*, NCBC (Grand Rapids: Wm. B. Eerdmans, 1980), 58.

15. J. Willis, "The Genre of Isaiah 5:1-7," *JBL* 96 (1977), 337–58. The intervening decade has not brought any decidedly different proposals.

16. J. William Whedbee, *Isaiah and Wisdom* (Nashville: Abingdon Press, 1971), 47.

17. RSV construed the construct chain *šîrat dôdî* as an objective genitive. However, this construal does not take seriously enough the definitiveness of the first member in the construct chain, i.e., *the* song of my beloved.

18. On the presence of narrative elements in Hebrew poetry, see Alter, *The Art of Biblical Poetry*, 27–61.

19. On Isa. 34:11-17 and curse language, see Delbert R. Hillers, *Treaty-*

Curses and the Old Testament Prophets, BibOr 16 (Rome: Pontifical Biblical Institute, 1964), 44–53.

20. Watson, *Classical Hebrew Poetry*, includes no reference to allegory as a literary technique used by ancient Israelite writers. Cf. Luis Alonso Schökel, *A Manual of Hebrew Poetics*, Subsidia Biblica 11 (Rome: Pontifical Biblical Institute, 1988), 109–10, for a brief discussion of allegory in the Hebrew Bible.

21. The diverse voices in the poem have not been fully recognized in one recent literary assessment of the poem: M. Lichtenstein, "Biblical Poetry," in *Back to the Sources. Reading the Classic Jewish Texts*, ed. Barry W. Holtz (New York: Summit Books, 1984), 122–23.

22. There is a continuing debate about the original location of these so-called superscriptions. It was customary in the ancient world to place the title page at the end in a postscript or colophon, (for example, Hab. 3:19); cf. Bruce K. Waltke, "Superscripts, Postscripts, or Both," *JBL* 110 (1991), 583–96.

23. Erhard Gerstenberger, *Psalms Part 1 with an Introduction to Cultic Poetry.* FOTL vol. 14, ed. Rolf Knierim and Gene M. Tucker (Grand Rapids: Wm. B. Eerdmans, 1988), 35.

24. There is an extensive bibliography on Psalm 1 beyond the commentaries. All of these are cataloged in a forthcoming article by K. H. Richards entitled "Deviate Grammar: The Poetics of Psalm One." Among the most important are John T. Willis, "Psalm 1—An Entity," *ZAW* 91 (1979), 381–401; J. A. Soggin, "Zum Ersten Psalm," *TZ* 23 (1967), 81–96; and P. Auffret, "Essai sur la structure littéraire du psaume 1," *BZ* New Series 22 (1978), 26–45.

25. H. Bardtke, "Erwägungen zu Psalm 1 und Psalm 2," in *Symbolae Biblicae et Mesopotamicae*, Festschrift F. M. T. de Liagre Böhl, ed. M. A. Beek et al. (Leiden: E. J. Brill, 1973), 1–18; W. H. Brownlee, "Psalms 1–2 as a Coronation Liturgy," *Bib* 52 (1971): 321–36; and E. Lipiński, "Macarismes et psaumes de congratulation," *RB* 75 (1968): 321–67.

26. Willis, "Psalm 1—An Entity," provides an extensive discussion of the evidence concerning those who have read Psalm 1 and Psalm 2 as one psalm, as well as the far greater evidence of those who have held Psalm 1 and Psalm 2 to be two distinct psalms.

27. James L. Mays, "The Place of Torah-Psalms in the Psalter," *JBL* 106 (1987), 4.

28. Many consider the text an introduction to the Psalter (Mays, Craigie, Kraus, and others), irrespective of whether or not they view Psalm 1 and Psalm 2 as separate literary units.

29. Cf. Tucker, *Form Criticism of the Old Testament*, 1–17, for a further definition of form criticism.

30. Gerstenberger, *Psalms Part 1 with an Introduction to Cultic Poetry*, says of some of the more specific psalms usually understood as wisdom genres that the designations of "torah psalm, song of retribution, or psalm of the two ways, are based not on form-critical observations but on content" (p. 43).

31. S. Bullough, "The Question of Metre in Psalm 1," *VT* 17 (1967), 42–49, is one of those who contend there is no meter but that Psalm 1 is "rhythmic prose" (p. 45). Craigie gives no rhythmic structure for Psalm 1 as he does for

most psalms in his commentary. O. Loretz, "Psalmenstudien," *UF* 3 (1971), 101–3, does provide an analysis of the rhythm, but there has been little advance beyond Hermann Gunkel's analysis in *Die Psalmen*, HKAT (Göttingen: Vandenhoeck & Ruprecht, 1926), 1. He understood the meter as follows:

v. 1	2 + 2 + 2
	3 + 3
v. 2	4 + 4
v. 3	4 + 4
v. 4	3 + 4
v. 5	4 + 3
v. 6	4 + 3

32. Alter has recently taken a similar position regarding the opening line, calling it an "introductory formula" or "virtual title" (*The Art of Biblical Poetry*, 114). There are a variety of theories about the initial line, but no one has taken this as a poetic marker for the poem.

33. W. Vogels, "A Structural Analysis of Ps 1," *Bib* 60 (1979), 413. He suggests that the "whole psalm is thus included between the first and last letters of the alphabet," forming an inclusion and alphabetical psalm. There are a number of alphabetic acrostics in the Psalter, including Psalms 25, 34, 57, and 119.

34. Norman K. Gottwald, *Studies in the Book of Lamentations*, rev. ed., SBT (London: SCM Press, 1962), 23–32, has an excellent discussion of the acrostic form. It seems clear that Babylonian acrostics have phonetic value, but few have taken this approach with Hebrew texts (pp. 28ff.).

35. See Watson, *Classical Hebrew Poetry*, 258, on similes; and see our discussion in chapter 4.

36. Miller, *Interpreting the Psalms*, 83.

37. There are extensive structural discussions best examined in Willis, "Psalm 1—An Entity." While his discussion comes under the category of "strophic structure," our position is not based on strophe. Chiastic structures within the Psalter as well as Psalm 1 have been investigated (cf. R. L. Alden, "Chiastic Psalms: A Study in the Mechanics of Hebrew Poetry in Psalms 1–50," *JETS* 17 [1974], 11–28).

38. Alter, *The Art of Biblical Poetry*, 116.

Selected Bibliography

Alonso Schökel, Luis. *A Manual of Hebrew Poetics.* Subsidia Biblica 11. Rome: Pontifical Biblical Institute, 1988.

Alter, Robert. *The Art of Biblical Poetry.* New York: Basic Books, 1985.

Berlin, Adele. *The Dynamics of Biblical Parallelism.* Bloomington, Ind.: Indiana University Press, 1985.

Chatman, Seymour. *A Theory of Meter.* Janua Linguarum, Series Minor, 36. The Hague: Mouton & Co., 1965.

Collins, Terence. *Line-Forms in Hebrew Poetry: A Grammatical Approach to the Stylistic Study of the Hebrew Prophets.* Studia Pohl, Series Maior, 17. Rome: Pontifical Biblical Institute, 1978.

Cross, Frank Moore and David Noel Freedman. *Studies in Ancient Yahwistic Poetry.* SBLDS 21. Missoula, Mont.: Scholars Press, 1975.

Dion, Paul E. *Hebrew Poetics: A Student's Guide.* Mississauga, Ont., Canada: Benben Publications, 1988.

Follis, Elaine, ed. *Directions in Biblical Hebrew Poetry.* JSOTSS 40. Sheffield, Eng.: JSOT Press, 1987.

Geller, Stephen A. *Parallelism in Early Biblical Poetry.* HSM 20. Missoula, Mont.: Scholars Press, 1979.

Gray, George B. *The Forms of Hebrew Poetry.* 1915. New York: KTAV, 1972.

Kugel, James L. *The Idea of Biblical Poetry: Parallelism and Its History.* New Haven: Yale University Press, 1981.

Lowth, Robert. *Lectures on the Sacred Poetry of the Hebrews.* London: S. Chadwick & Co., 1847.

Miller, Patrick D., Jr. "Poetry and Interpretation," *Interpreting the Psalms,* 29–47. Philadelphia: Fortress Press, 1986.

O'Connor, Michael. *Hebrew Verse Structure.* Winona Lake, Ind.: Eisenbrauns, 1980.

Pardee, Dennis. *Ugaritic and Hebrew Poetic Parallelism: A Trial Cut ('nt I and Proverbs 2).* VTSup 39. Leiden: E. J. Brill, 1988.

Preminger, Alex, et al., eds. *The Princeton Handbook of Poetic Terms.* Princeton: Princeton University Press, 1986.

Stuart, Douglas. *Studies in Early Hebrew Meter.* HSM 13. Missoula, Mont.: Scholars Press, 1976.

Watson, Wilfred G. E. *Classical Hebrew Poetry: A Guide to Its Techniques.* JSOTSS 26. Sheffield, Eng.: JSOT Press, 1986.

Author Index

Scripture Index